Business Principles and Management

Eleventh Edition
Anniversary Edition

Volume 2

Kenneth E. Everard
James L. Burrow

THOMSON

NELSON

For more information contact Thomson Nelson
1120 Birchmount Road,
Scarborough, Ontario, M1K 5G4.
Or you can visit our internet site at
http://www.nelson.com

For permission to use material from this text or product, contact us by
Tel 1-800-730-2214
Fax 1-800-730-2215
www.thomsonrights.com

This textbook is a Nelson custom publication. Because your instructor has chosen to produce a custom publication, you pay only for material that you will use in your course.

Cover Photo: Stockbyte

ISBN-13: 978-0-17-646273-4
ISBN-10: 0-17-646273-2

Consists of:

*Business Principles and Management,
Eleventh Edition Anniversary Edition*
Kenneth E. Everard
James L. Burrow
ISBN 0-538-43590-9, © 2004

Contents

· ·

Business Principles and Management

Volume 2

· ·

UNIT TWO

FORMS of BUSINESS OWNERSHIP and the LAW

CHAPTERS

Recent changes in the economy have stimulated increased interest in being one's own boss. The downsizing of large corporations has displaced millions of workers and managers. Many of these employees have taken the trauma of being laid off and turned it into a self-employment opportunity, frequently financed in large part by severance pay or an early retirement bonus.

Stephen P. Robbins
Managing Today, 1997

PROPRIETORSHIPS AND PARTNERSHIPS

OBJECTIVES

5-1	Describe characteristics of successful entrepreneurs.
5-2	Outline responsibilities of owning your own business.
5-3	List advantages and disadvantages of proprietorships.
5-4	List advantages and disadvantages of partnerships.
5-5	Describe legal points to consider when selecting a name for a business.

ONE WAY TO START A BUSINESS

ancy Watanabe wondered about the rest of her life as she sat in front of her computer. Was she too young to even consider starting her own business? Was the whole idea of opening a small computer rental business ridiculous for a nineteen-year-old? "My father would be proud if he knew my dream of investing the inherited money to start a business," she thought to herself. "If only he were here to show me what to do. Fortunately, the library and the Internet have plenty of information on how to get started."

Nancy continued thinking to herself. "I've learned plenty during the last several weeks,
reading and talking with my neighbor who runs the local Taco Bell fast-food business. Working as a cashier and computer salesperson in the local computer store while in high school also gave me experience. Yet, there's so much I don't know. I never hired anyone or kept the books. But the idea is so exciting. Will people stop at . . . Nancy's Computer Rentals . . . for an extra computer during busy times or while they wait for their broken computer to be repaired?" Nancy turned back to her Web browser. "Did I just name my store?" she asked, smiling to herself.

Many people have dreamed about owning their own businesses. The idea may have crossed your mind, too. These dreams often start as simple ideas. Some of the dreamers with practical ideas do form businesses. That is how many well-known founders of large businesses got started. Hundreds of young entrepreneurs have started their own firms, including Dell Computer's Michael Dell, Microsoft's Bill Gates, and Amazon.com's Jeff Bezos.

Most businesses begin with one owner. But some firms start with two or more owners. One person, or a group of people, invests in a business with the hope of becoming successful owners. This chapter will examine the basic elements, advantages, and disadvantages of starting a business alone or with others.

■ CHARACTERISTICS OF ENTREPRENEURS

You learned earlier that an entrepreneur is a person who assumes the risk of starting, owning, and operating a business for the purpose of making a profit. Although individuals form businesses to earn a profit by providing consumers with a desired product or service, they often must invest months or even years of hard work before they earn a profit. About half of all new businesses end within the first five to six years. Businesses often fail for financial reasons, but many closings of young firms occur because the owners are not well suited to be entrepreneurs. But while successful entrepreneurs are all uniquely different, they also have some common personal characteristics.

Some people would rather work for others, while other people prefer to work for themselves. Entrepreneurs who prefer self-employment enjoy the freedom and independence that come from being their own bosses and from making their own decisions. Even when their businesses are not immediately successful, they do not give up. In fact, some entrepreneurs who are eventually successful often experience unsuccessful business start-ups. However, they learn from their mistakes and start over.

Entrepreneurs are self-starters who have plenty of energy and enjoy working on their own. They like to take charge of situations and usually work hard and for long periods in order to meet their goals. Entrepreneurs are also creative thinkers, often coming up with new ideas and new ways to solve problems. Most successful small business owners like people and people like them. As a result, they are often community leaders.

Prosperous entrepreneurs have other common characteristics. Generally, they obtain work experience in the types of businesses they launch. The person who starts a computer store, for example, will usually have taken some computer courses and will have worked for a business that makes, sells, or services computers. In addition to appropriate work experience, successful business owners are well informed about financial, marketing, and legal matters.

There is no magic age for starting a business. Teenagers, parents of teenagers, and retirees have all started successful firms. In recent years, increasing numbers of women, Asian-Americans, Hispanics, and African-Americans of all ages have opened their own firms. To start your own business, you need adequate funds, a general knowledge about business, some work experience, and a business opportunity.

One of the very first decisions a budding business owner must make is what legal form of ownership to adopt. The form of ownership

FACTS AND FIGURES

The U.S. economy is dominated by family businesses. According to some estimates, as many as 90 percent of all businesses, including the majority of small- and medium-sized companies, are owned by families.

ILLUSTRATION 5-1

An entrepreneur assumes the risk of starting and operating a business for the purpose of making a profit. What are some personal characteristics of entrepreneurs?

selected depends on several factors, such as the nature and size of the business, the capital needed, the tax laws, and the financial responsibility the owner is willing to assume. Two legal forms of business ownership—proprietorships and partnerships—are presented in this chapter. Also presented in this chapter is the selection of a legal name for a business. But first, let's investigate the challenging responsibilities that entrepreneurs face.

GETTING A BUSINESS STARTED

Starting a business entails many more responsibilities than simply being an employee. Assume, for example, that you are employed as a delivery person. Your duties include making pickups and deliveries. After obtaining several years of valuable work experience, you decide to start your own delivery service. You need to create a plan and to develop an awareness of your responsibilities as the owner of a business.

PREPARE A BUSINESS PLAN

Before starting a business, you need to prepare a business plan. A **business plan** is a written document that describes the nature of the business, the company's goals and objectives, and how they will be achieved. The business plan requires a great deal of careful thought. Most plans include those items shown in Figure 5-1.

Developing a business plan will help you see more clearly the risks and responsibilities involved in starting a business, and will help you decide whether you really want to do it. Writing down your strategies for achieving your goals can give you confidence that your business can succeed. Your plan can also inspire the confidence of others with whom you will deal. Bankers, for instance, will ask to see your plan if you wish to borrow startup funds. They will have greater assurance when they see how carefully you have considered potential problems and solutions before launching your new enterprise. Equally important will be your own conviction that your business will thrive. Too many people who enter business fail for three reasons: (1) they did not prepare a business plan, (2) their plan was unrealistic, or (3) they wrote the plan only because the moneylender, such as a bank, required it. To be successful, you need to start with a well-designed, realistic plan.

ASSUME THE RESPONSIBILITIES OF BUSINESS OWNERSHIP

By developing a workable business plan, entrepreneurs become aware of their risks. As a result, they may be able to anticipate problems and take preventive action. The business plan also causes the aspiring business owner to become more realistic about the responsibilities of ownership.

FIGURE 5-1

Elements of a Business Plan

NATURE OF THE BUSINESS

- Detailed description of products and/or services
- Estimation of risk based on analysis of the industry
- Size of business
- Location of business
- Background of entrepreneur(s)

GOALS AND OBJECTIVES

- Basic results expected in the short and long run
- Results expressed in terms of sales volume or profits

MARKETING PLAN

- Customers and their demand for the product or service
- Prices for the product or service
- Comparison of product or service with competitors

FINANCIAL PLAN

- Investment needed to start and maintain the business
- Projected income, expenses, and profit
- Cash start-up and cash flow needs

ORGANIZATIONAL PLAN

- Legal form of ownership
- Legal factors—licenses, leases, contracts
- Organization chart
- Job descriptions and employee skills needed
- Physical facilities—buildings, equipment, tools

As the owner of your new delivery service, you have duties that include not only pickups and deliveries but also many other responsibilities. Even if you run the business from your home, you will have added expenses for an office, a garage, a computer and printer, and communication devices such as a fax, cell phone, and answering machine. You must find customers, persuade those customers to pay a fair price for your services, and collect from those customers. Furthermore, you must assume responsibility for damage that may occur to your merchandise. You will have to pay fees for various licenses, taxes, insurance premiums, gasoline, van repairs, and other operating expenses. It may also be necessary to hire, train, and supervise employees.

Aspiring entrepreneurs should carefully consider the responsibilities of ownership before opening a business. These tasks are welcome challenges for some people, but may seem like overwhelming burdens to others. People who enjoy being leaders and enjoy making decisions find great satisfaction in owning a business. Ownership offers opportunities to make decisions and to experience other rewards. Some of these rewards will be identified in the section that follows.

PROPRIETORSHIP

The most common form of business organization is the proprietorship, of which there are over 16 million in this country. A business owned and managed by one person is known as a **sole proprietorship,** or a **proprietorship,** and the owner-manager is the **proprietor.** In addition to owning and managing the business, the proprietor often performs the day-to-day tasks that make a business successful, with the help of hired employees. Under the proprietorship form of organization, the owner furnishes expertise, money, and management. For assuming these responsibilities, the owner is entitled to all profits earned by the business.

Provided that no debts are owed, a proprietor has full claim to the *assets*—property owned by the business. If the proprietor has business debts, however, **creditors** (those to whom money is owed) have first claim against the assets. Figure 5-2 presents a simple financial statement of Jennifer York, who is the proprietor of a small retail grocery store and fruit market.

This simple financial statement, known as a *statement of financial position,* or *balance sheet,* shows that the assets of the business are valued at $218,400. Since York has *liabilities* (money owed by a business) amounting to $14,400, the balance sheet shows her capital as $204,000 ($218,400 minus $14,400). In accounting, the terms *capital, net worth,* and *equity* are interchangeable and are defined as assets less liabilities. If there are profits, York gets the total amount. She must also absorb losses. Since she owns the land and the building, she does not have to pay rent, although she must pay the cost of maintenance and taxes for the property.

ADVANTAGES OF PROPRIETORSHIPS

The fact that almost three out of four businesses are proprietorships indicates that this form of organization has definite advantages. Can you list any of the advantages before reading further?

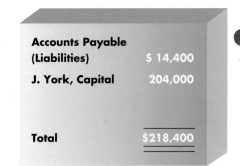

ASSETS

Cash	$ 17,760
Merchandise	31,680
Equipment	24,960
Land & Buildings	144,000
Total	$218,400

CLAIMS AGAINST ASSETS

Accounts Payable (Liabilities)	$ 14,400
J. York, Capital	204,000
Total	$218,400

FIGURE 5-2

Jennifer York's Balance Sheet

OWNER IS BOSS   There is a great deal of pride and satisfaction in being one's own boss and being responsible only to oneself. The proprietor can be inventive and creative in working out ideas to make the business a success.

OWNER RECEIVES ALL PROFITS   Very closely related to this first advantage is the fact that all the profits belong to the sole proprietor. As a result, the owner is more likely to work overtime and to think continually of how the business can operate more efficiently.

OWNER PERSONALLY KNOWS EMPLOYEES AND CUSTOMERS   Because most proprietorships are small, the proprietor and the employees know one another personally. This relationship can lead to mutual understanding and a feeling of "family" as employer and employees work side-by-side in daily business activities. Sole proprietors often develop close relationships with their customers as well.

OWNER CAN ACT QUICKLY IN DECISION MAKING   Sole proprietors can make decisions without consulting others, so they can act promptly when the need arises. If an unusual opportunity to buy merchandise or equipment occurs, or if the owner wishes to change the location of the business or to sell on credit terms rather than on a cash basis, there are no dissenting partners to stop such action. Thus, the management of a proprietorship is flexible and can adjust rapidly to changing conditions.

OWNER IS FREE FROM RED TAPE   A sole proprietor can usually begin or end business activities without legal formality. Sole proprietorships can be organized without a lot of legal documents or government red tape. In some types of businesses, however, such as a restaurant, it is necessary to obtain a license before operations can begin.

OWNER USUALLY PAYS LESS INCOME TAX THAN A CORPORATION   In most sole proprietorships, the income tax is often less than in the corporation type of business, which is explained in the next chapter.

CAREER CONNECTION

ENTREPRENEUR

"Entrepreneur" is a long word that simply refers to someone who owns, operates, and takes the risk of a business venture. Today, millions of small businesses contribute billions of dollars to the United States economy. There are many opportunities for entrepreneurs in all types of businesses: manufacturing, wholesaling, retailing, and services.

Would entrepreneurship be right for you? Successful entrepreneurs are independent and self-confident; they have determination and perseverance; they are goal-oriented; they set high standards for themselves; they are creative; and they are able to act quickly.

Entrepreneurs are their own bosses and can choose a business that interests them. However, entrepreneurship is risky. Small businesses face the possibility of going out of business or losing money. In addition, entrepreneurs work long hours and face uncertain incomes. As you continue your study of business principles and management, think about whether you have what it takes to make it as an entrepreneur.

For more career information about entrepreneurs, check your library or the Internet for resources.

■ DISADVANTAGES OF PROPRIETORSHIPS

There are many advantages to owning your own business. However, there are also some disadvantages facing the sole proprietor.

OWNER MAY LACK NECESSARY SKILLS AND ABILITIES   Each person has special skills and abilities. One person may excel at selling. Another person may be more talented at purchasing goods or keeping records. Still a third person may be superior at supervising employees. All of these activities are important to the success of a business, but the proprietor is likely to be weak in one or more areas. No one can do everything well. It is therefore easy to understand why some proprietorships end in failure within a short time.

OWNER MAY LACK FUNDS   Additional funds (capital) are often needed for emergencies. Financial assistance on a large scale may be difficult to obtain by a single owner. Therefore, the expansion of the business may be slowed because of the owner's lack of capital.

OWNER BEARS ALL LOSSES   Sole proprietors assume a great deal of risk. While sole owners receive all the profits of the business, they also bear all the losses if the business fails. If the business fails and the owner is unable to pay the debts of the business, the creditors have a claim against the owner's personal assets, not just the assets of the business. The sole entrepreneur may therefore lose not only the money invested in the enterprise but also personal possessions, such as a car or home.

ILLNESS OR DEATH MAY CLOSE THE BUSINESS   The continuing operation of a sole proprietorship depends on the longevity of the proprietor. If the owner becomes unable to work because of illness or dies, the business would have to close.

■ BUSINESSES SUITED TO BEING PROPRIETORSHIPS

The kind of business that is primarily concerned with providing personal services is well suited to the proprietorship form of organization. Dentists, accountants, landscape gardeners, carpenters, painters, barbers, beauty salons, Web site developers, and computer *consultants* (experts) are examples of businesses frequently organized as proprietorships.

Another type of business that seems to be well adapted to the proprietorship form of business is the one that sells merchandise or services on a small scale. Newspaper and magazine stands, roadside markets, fast food and family restaurants, flower shops, gasoline stations, small grocery stores, fish markets, and many Web-based businesses that sell crafts, gourmet foods, or grocery delivery services are examples. In general, the type of business that can be operated suitably as a proprietorship is one that (1) is small enough to be managed by the proprietor or a few people hired by the proprietor and (2) does not require a large amount of capital.

■ PARTNERSHIP

Jennifer York, who operates the proprietorship mentioned earlier, is faced with the problem of expanding her business. She has run the business successfully for over ten years. She sees new opportunities in the community for increasing her business, but she does not wish to assume full responsibility for the undertaking. She realizes that the expansion of the business will place on her considerable financial and managerial responsibilities. She also realizes that in order to expand she needs additional capital, but she does not want to borrow the money. Because of these reasons, she has decided that it will be wise to change her business from a proprietorship to a **partnership,** a business owned by two or more people.

Robert Burton operates an adjoining bakery, where he bakes fresh bread and pastries daily. He has proven to be honest and to have considerable business ability. Combining the two businesses could result in more customers for both groceries and fresh baked goods. Customers who have been coming to the bake shop may become grocery customers also. And those who have been buying at the grocery and fruit market may become customers of bakery products. A discussion between York and Burton leads to a tentative agreement to form a partnership if a third person can be found who will invest enough cash to remodel both stores to form one large store and to purchase additional equipment. The financial statement of Burton's business is shown in Figure 5-3.

The net worth of Burton's business is $153,600. In other words, after deducting the amount of his liabilities ($7,200) from the total value of his assets ($160,800), his business is worth $153,600. According to Jen-

ASSETS

CLAIMS AGAINST ASSETS

Cash	$ 10,560
Merchandise	3,600
Equipment	26,640
Land & Buildings	120,000
Total	$160,800

Accounts Payable (Liabilities)	$ 7,200
R. Burton, Capital	153,600
Total	$160,800

FIGURE 5-3

Balance Sheet for Robert Burton

nifer York's balance sheet in Figure 5-2, her business is worth $204,000. In order to have an equal investment in the partnership, Burton must invest an additional $50,400 in cash.

They find Lu Chan, a person with accounting experience, who has $144,000 and is able to borrow the remaining $60,000 to become an equal partner. The partnership agreement, shown in Figure 5-6, is then written and signed by York, Burton, and Chan.

Once the partnership is formed, a statement of financial position (balance sheet) must be prepared. This statement shows the total assets, liabilities, and capital of the owners at the start of the business. The partnership's balance sheet is shown in Figure 5-4. Each asset category on the combined balance sheet (merchandise, equipment, and land and buildings) as well as the accounts payable liability category are the totals of these categories from Burton's and York's businesses. The cash category combines the cash from both businesses plus Chan's cash investment of $204,000.

A key factor in the success of a partnership is for the partners to clearly agree upon each person's responsibilities. York, Burton, and Chan divide their duties: York supervises the grocery department, Burton supervises the bake shop and meat department, and Chan handles the finances, inventory, and records.

ASSETS

CLAIMS AGAINST ASSETS

Cash	$282,720
Merchandise	35,280
Equipment	51,600
Land & Buildings	264,000
Total	$633,600

Accounts Payable (Liabilities)	$ 21,600
J. York, Capital	204,000
R. Burton, Capital	204,000
L. Chan, Capital	204,000
Total	$633,600

FIGURE 5-4

Balance Sheet for York, Burton, and Chan at Startup

ASSETS

CLAIMS AGAINST ASSETS

ASSETS		CLAIMS AGAINST ASSETS	
Cash	$ 240,000	Accounts Payable (Liabilities)	$ 74,900
Merchandise	60,000	J. York, Capital	221,700
Equipment	90,000	R. Burton, Capital	221,700
Land & Buildings	350,000	L. Chan, Capital	221,700
Total	$740,000	Total	$740,000

During the year the three partners combine the stores, remodel them, buy new equipment, and open for business. The financial statement at the end of the year, shown in Figure 5-5, shows the results of the new partnership.

Has the partnership had a successful year? Each partner has received a salary of $5,000 a month (according to the terms of the partnership agreement). In addition, the capital or net worth of each partner has increased from $204,000 to $221,700 as a result of profits made during the year. This increase in the total capital from $612,000 ($204,000 times 3) to $665,100 ($221,700 times 3) amounts to $53,100 and is an increase of nearly 8.7 percent. Chan, who borrowed some of the money for his investment, had to pay 7 percent interest to the lender. His investment in the partnership brought him a return that is more than the interest on his loan.

ADVANTAGES OF PARTNERSHIPS

Many businesses are organized as partnerships at the very beginning. Figure 5-6 shows a partnership agreement. There are nearly 1.6 million businesses operating as partnerships in the United States, which is small in comparison to sole proprietorships. While most partnerships have only two or three partners, there is no limit set on the number of partners. Some businesses have as many as ten or more partners. Some of the advantages of partnerships are discussed below.

SKILLS AND ABILITIES POOLED   A partnership is likely to be operated more efficiently than a proprietorship, because a partnership can draw on the skills of two or more people, instead of just one. One partner may have special sales ability; another may have an aptitude for buying the right kind, quality, and quantity of merchandise. One partner may propose a change in the business; another partner may be able to point out disadvantages in the plan and suggest changes that were not initially apparent. In a sole proprietorship, the single owner must have skills in all key business areas or be able to hire people with the needed skills for the business to succeed.

FACTS AND FIGURES

"Partners" can be classified in a variety of ways. For example, a silent partner may be known to the public as a partner, but takes no active part in management. A secret partner is not known to the public as a partner, yet participates in management. A dormant partner is neither known to the public as a partner nor active in management.

Partnership Agreement

FIGURE 5-6

A clearly written and understood partnership agreement can prevent problems later.

This contract, made and entered into on the first day of June, 20-- by and between Jennifer L. York, of Buffalo, New York, party of the first part, Robert R. Burton, of Buffalo, New York, party of the second part, Lu Chan of Niagara Falls, New York, party of the third part:

Witnesseth: That the said parties have this day formed a partnership for the purpose of engaging in and conducting a retail grocery-fruit-meat market and bakery under the following stipulations, which are made a part of the contract:

First: The said partnership is to continue for a term of ten years from date hereof.

Second: The business shall be conducted under the firm name of Y, B, & C Fine Foods, at 4467 Goodson Street, Buffalo, New York.

Third: The investments are as follows: Jennifer L. York: Cash, $17,760; Merchandise, $31,680; Equipment, $24,960; Land and Buildings, $144,000; Total Assets, $218,400; less Accounts Payable, $14,400, equals Net Investment, $204,000. Robert R. Burton: Cash, $10,560; Merchandise, $3,600; Equipment, $26,640; Land and Buildings, $120,000; Total Assets, $160,800, less Accounts Payable, $7,200, equals Net Investment, $153,000. Lu Chan: Cash, $204,000.

Fourth: All profits or losses arising from said business are to be shared equally.

Fifth: Each partner is to devote his or her entire time and attention to the business and to engage in no other business enterprise without the written consent of the others.

Sixth: Each partner is to have a salary of $5,000 a month, the same to be withdrawn at such time as he or she may elect. No partner is to withdraw from the business an amount in excess of his or her salary without the written consent of the others.

Seventh: The duties of each partner are defined as follows: Jennifer L. York is to supervise the grocery-fruit-vegetable departments. Robert R. Burton is to supervise the bakery and meat departments. Lu Chan is to manage finances, inventory, and records.

Eighth: No partner is to become surety for anyone without the written consent of the others.

Ninth: In case of the death, incapacity, or withdrawal of one partner, the business is to be conducted for the remainder of the fiscal year by the surviving partners, the profits for the year allocated to the withdrawing partner to be determined by the ratio of the time he or she was a partner during the year to the whole year.

Tenth: In case of dissolution the assets are to be divided in the ratio of the capital invested at the time of dissolution.

In Witness Whereof, the parties aforesaid have hereunto set their hands and affixed their seals on the day and year above written.

In the presence of:

.... (Seal)

. . . . (Seal)

. . . . (Seal)

SOURCES OF CAPITAL INCREASED   A new business needs capital to buy the equipment, inventory, and office space needed to get started. Often two or more people can supply more capital than one person can. When the business needs to expand, generally several partners can obtain the additional capital needed for the expansion more easily than one person can.

ILLUSTRATION 5-3

A partnership is a business owned by two or more persons. Why might a partnership be operated more efficiently than a proprietorship?

CREDIT POSITION IMPROVED   The partnership usually has a better credit reputation than the sole proprietorship. This is often true because more than one owner is responsible for the ownership and management of the business.

CONTRIBUTION OF GOODWILL   Each partner is likely to have a large personal following. Some people will be more likely to do business with the newly formed partnership because they know one of the owners. This is known as *goodwill*.

INCREASED CONCERN IN BUSINESS MANAGEMENT   Each owner of the business will have a greater interest in the firm as a partner than as an employee. Much of this is due to the greater financial responsibility each person has as a partner.

LESS TAX BURDEN THAN CORPORATIONS   Partnerships usually have a tax advantage over corporations. You will learn more about this in Chapter 6. Partnerships prepare a federal income tax report but do not pay a tax on their profits, as do corporations. However, partners must pay a personal income tax on their individual share of the profit.

REDUCTION IN COMPETITION   Two or more proprietors in the same line of business may become one organization by forming a partnership. This move may substantially decrease, or even eliminate, competition.

RETIREMENT FROM MANAGEMENT   A sole proprietor may wish to retire. However, the proprietor may not want to close the business. In such a case, the owner may form a partnership and allow the new owner to manage the business.

OPERATING ECONOMIES   It is often possible to operate more efficiently by combining two or more businesses. In such a case, certain operating expenses—such as advertising, supplies, equipment, fuel, and rent—can be reduced.

MANAGEMENT CLOSE-UP

BEN AND JERRY'S HOMEMADE, INC.

On May 5, 1978, Ben Cohen and Jerry Greenfield formed an ice cream parlor partnership in a renovated gas station in Burlington, Vermont. The two former seventh-grade buddies, who used top-quality ingredients, were delighted by their early success. Yet, to survive in those initial days they needed to improve sales to cover expenses.

The business grew rapidly, but they had early concerns about getting too large. When the business was small, they enjoyed working alongside employees while making and experimenting with new products and flavors. But as the business grew, they began to grow apart from their employees and started to feel as if they were losing the enjoyment experienced during the start-up days. Job fulfillment satisfied them more than profits.

They tried to resist further expansion but knew the business either had to grow or fade away. Jerry retired. Another entrepreneur, however, convinced Ben that he could serve employees and the public while continuing to expand. With a new focus, Jerry rejoined Ben. Together they modified the firm's goals to expand their product line and also improve the quality of life for employees and all of society.

Today, Ben and Jerry's has over 700 employees and produces enough flavors to satisfy millions of customers. The company makes, distributes, and sells super-premium ice cream, sorbet, and yogurt to supermarkets, restaurants, and over 140 franchised and company outlets in highly populated states and nine foreign countries. Sales exceed $200 million yearly.

Ben and Jerry remain committed to their employees. They achieved national recognition for developing a proud and productive workforce. The emphasis given workers was once reflected in their 7-to-1 rule that prevented any employee—including managers—from earning more than seven times what the lowest-paid employee earns. Recently the rule changed, however, because the pay scale for attracting excellent top executives was too low.

One important thing has not changed—Ben and Jerry's commitment to social responsibility. Each year a sizable percentage of profits goes to charities and social causes. Donations to charities, art, and public musical concerts are common. Ben and Jerry—an unusual pair of innovative partners—have created a unique style of doing business.

THINK CRITICALLY

1. At the outset, was Ben and Jerry's business typical for a new enterprise? Give reasons for your answer.
2. Why did Ben and Jerry want their company to remain small?
3. If the lowest-paid employee earned $15,000 a year, what would the maximum salary be for the highest-paid manager under the 7-to-1 rule? Why might this manager be unhappy with this rule?
4. Determine what the company is doing today to fulfill its social obligations and also find out about its new products, sales, and profits.

■ DISADVANTAGES OF PARTNERSHIPS

While there are many advantages of partnerships, there are also disadvantages, as described below.

UNLIMITED FINANCIAL LIABILITY   According to law, each member of the partnership has an **unlimited financial liability** for all the debts of the business. If some of the partners are unable to pay their share, one partner may have to pay all the debts.

Suppose that the partnership of York, Burton, and Chan failed and that after all the business assets were changed into cash and used to pay business debts, the partnership still owed creditors $18,000. Legally, the partners must pay these debts from their own personal savings or sell personal property, such as their car or house, to obtain the cash to pay off the debts. In this case, each partner should contribute $6,000 ($18,000 divided by 3) from their personal assets. But if, say, Burton and Chan did not have the $6,000 in personal assets to pay their portions, York would be legally responsible for using her personal savings and property to pay the entire $18,000.

DISAGREEMENT AMONG PARTNERS   There is always danger of disagreement among partners. The majority of the partners may want to change the nature of the business but are unable to do so because one partner refuses. For example, a partnership may have been formed to conduct a retail business selling audio equipment. After a while, the majority of the partners may think it wise to add cellular phones to their line of merchandise. The change may benefit the business. However, as long as one partner disagrees, the partnership cannot make the change. Furthermore, partners sometimes feel that they are not properly sharing in the management. This situation may cause disagreements that could hurt the business. Such a condition can be partly prevented if the partnership agreement states the duties of each partner.

EACH PARTNER BOUND BY CONTRACTS OF OTHERS   Each partner is bound by the partnership contracts made by any partner if such contracts apply to the ordinary operations of the business. If one partner commits to a contract in the name of the partnership, all partners are legally bound by it, whether they think the contract is good for the business or not. Disagreements can eventually lead to partnership failure.

UNCERTAIN LIFE   The life of a partnership is uncertain. Sometimes when partners draw up a partnership contract, they specify a definite length of time, such as ten years, for the existence of the business. Should one partner die, however, the partnership ends. The deceased partner may have been the principal manager; and, as a result of his or her death, the business may suffer. The heirs of the deceased partner may demand an unfair price from the surviving partners for the share of the deceased partner. Or the heirs may insist upon ending the partnership quickly to obtain the share belonging to the dead partner. In the latter case, the assets that are sold may not bring a fair price; and, as a result, all the partners suffer a loss. A partnership can carry insurance on the life of a partner to provide money to purchase the share of a partner who dies. Under the laws of most states, the bankruptcy of any partner or the admission of a new partner are other causes that may bring a sudden end to the partnership.

LIMITED SOURCES OF CAPITAL   The contributions of the partners, the earnings of the business, and the money that can be borrowed limit the amount of funds that a partnership can obtain. It is difficult for a partnership to obtain enough capital to operate a large business unless each member of the partnership is wealthy or unless there are many partners. Too many partners, however, may cause inefficient operations.

UNSATISFACTORY DIVISION OF PROFITS   Sometimes the partnership profits are not divided fairly according to the contributions of the individual partners. Partners should agree up front on how to divide profits according to the amount of labor, expertise, and capital each partner is expected to contribute. The partnership should then specify the agreed-upon division in the partnership agreement, such as 60 percent to one partner and 40 percent to another. If no provision is made in the agreement, the law requires an equal division of the profits. Then if, say, one partner contributes more time, expertise, or labor to the business than do the others, this partner may feel that he or she deserves more than an equal share of the profit.

DIFFICULTY IN WITHDRAWING FROM PARTNERSHIP   If a partner wishes to sell his or her interest in the business, it may be difficult to do so. Even if a buyer is found, the buyer may not be acceptable to the other partners.

■ LIMITED PARTNERSHIPS

In an ordinary (general) partnership, each partner is personally liable for all the debts incurred by the partnership. The laws of some states, however, permit the formation of a **limited partnership,** which restricts the liability of a partner to the amount of the partner's investment. In a limited partnership, not all partners have unlimited financial liability for the partnership debts. However, at least one partner must be a general partner who has unlimited liability. In many states, the name of a limited partner may not be included in the firm name.

Under the Uniform Limited Partnership Act, the states have created similar regulations for controlling limited partnerships. For example, the law requires that a certificate of limited partnership be filed in a public office of record and that proper notice be given to each creditor with whom the limited partnership does business. If these requirements are not fulfilled, the limited partners have unlimited liability in the same manner as a general partner.

The limited partnership is a useful form of business organization in situations where one person wishes to invest in a business but does not have the time or interest to participate actively in its management. Any business that is formed as a proprietorship can usually be formed as a limited partnership.

■ BUSINESSES SUITED TO BEING PARTNERSHIPS

The partnership form of organization is common among businesses that furnish more than one kind of product or service. Each partner usually looks after a specialized phase of the business. For example, car dealers often have sales and service departments. One partner may handle the sale of new cars, and another partner may be in charge of servicing and repairing cars. Still another partner could be in charge of used car sales or of the accounting and financial side of the business. Similarly, if a business operates in more than one location, each partner can be in charge of a specific location. Businesses that operate longer than the usual eight hours a day, such as the retail food business advertised in Figure 5-7, find the partnership organization desirable. Each partner can be in charge for part of the day.

Partnerships are also common in the same types of businesses that are formed as proprietorships, particularly in selling goods and services to consumers. It is especially popular in professional services, such as lawyers, doctors, accountants, and financial consultants. Internet businesses have been formed as partnerships as well. Good faith, together with reasonable care in the exercise of management duties, is required of all partners in a business.

ILLUSTRATION 5-4

A limited partnership restricts the liability of a partner for the amount of the partner's investment. Why might a limited partnership be a useful form of business organization?

FIGURE 5-7

An Advertisement Used to Announce the Opening of the Y, B, and C Partnership

■ BUSINESS NAME

A proprietorship or a partnership may be conducted under the name or names of the owner or owners. In many states, the law prohibits the use of *and Company* or *& Co.* unless such identification indicates additional partners. For example, if there are only two partners, it is not permissible to use a firm name such as Jones, Smith & Co., because that name indicates at least three partners. The name or names included in the term "Company" must be identified by registration at a public recording office, usually the county clerk's office. Usually one can do business under a trade, or artificial name, such as The Superior Shoe Store or W-W Manufacturing Company. Likewise, proper registration is usually required so that creditors may know everyone who is responsible for the business. Operating under a trade name, therefore, does not reduce the owners' liability to creditors.

CHAPTER CONCEPTS

- Most small businesses begin with one or a few owners. These new entrepreneurs often possess certain characteristics that help assure their success, such as the strong need to be boss, to make their own decisions, and to take reasonable risks. To aid their success, however, they must prepare a carefully developed business plan.

- A sole proprietorship, or proprietorship, is a business owned and operated by one person. It is the most popular form of business ownership. Many small retail and service businesses are single-owner firms because they are the easiest to start. The proprietor has other advantages, such as the power to make all decisions and make them quickly if needed, receive all profits, pay less in taxes than corporations, and know employees and customers personally. A proprietor also has few legal obstacles in starting a business.

- Proprietorships have a few critical disadvantages, such as lacking skills or knowledge needed for performing all key business tasks, lacking funds for expansion, surviving when major financial losses occur, and closing should illness or death occur.

- A partnership is a business owned by two or more people. Partnerships have key advantages over sole proprietorships. For example, multiple owners can contribute more capital to start or expand and more skills to improve business efficiency. Also, more partners can obtain more credit from banks and other sources. Because partnerships are larger than proprietorships, they can compete better. Finally, a partnership need not close because of the retirement of an owner.

- Partnerships have several major disadvantages. Each partner has unlimited financial liability for all business debts. And each partner is responsible for the contracts made by other partners. Other problems can arise when breaking up a partnership, deciding how to divide profits, and lacking the capital needed to expand.

- Like proprietorships, small retail stores are often partnerships, as are professional service businesses, such as doctors, lawyers, and accountants. Some partnerships may have limited partners. A limited partner often does not participate in running a business and has limited liability. However, one or more of the members of a partnership must be an ordinary (general) partner with unlimited liability.

BUILD VOCABULARY POWER

Define the following terms and concepts.

1. business plan
2. sole proprietorship (proprietorship)
3. proprietor
4. creditors
5. partnership
6. unlimited financial liability
7. limited partnership

REVIEW FACTS

1. What are two common legal forms of business ownership?
2. How will a good business plan help someone successfully open a new business?
3. What types of people enjoy the responsibilities of business ownership?
4. List the major advantages of proprietorships.
5. List the major disadvantages of proprietorships.
6. Which kinds of businesses are most suited to the proprietorship form of business ownership?
7. List the major advantages of partnerships.
8. List the major disadvantages of partnerships.
9. Under what types of situations is a limited partnership useful?
10. Why is it necessary for proprietorships and partnerships to register their company names with local authorities?

DISCUSS IDEAS

1. Your friend followed your advice and made a business plan to create a new business called Cookies to Go. You noticed she did not include a marketing plan and you mention it. She then says, "Everyone likes cookies. My prices depend on how much it costs to make each type of cookie. And there isn't a cookie store within three blocks of where I plan to locate my business. How could I go wrong?" List questions that should be answered in the marketing plan that would make your friend give more thought to her decision.

2. You have been working part-time and summers at a local service station during your school years. You have performed just about every major task from pumping gas to repairing cars and even handling some of the bookkeeping. Discuss how your responsibilities as an employee will change if you become the owner of the station.

3. A sole proprietor has no partners to participate in making decisions. What disadvantages could result from not having partners help in the decision-making process?

4. If a proprietorship needs additional capital but the owner cannot furnish it from personal funds, from what sources might capital be obtained?

5. Why should a partnership agreement include a clause such as the fifth clause shown in Figure 5-6?

6. Why should a partnership agreement include a clause such as the seventh clause shown in Figure 5-6?

7. Why should a partnership agreement be in writing?

8. A partner signed a partnership contract for television advertising while the other two partners were on vacation. Upon returning,

the vacationing partners claimed that the partnership was not bound to the contract because both of them disapproved of television advertising. Was the partnership legally bound?

9. What effect is there on the life of a partnership when (a) a partner dies, (b) a partner quits, and (c) a new partner is added?

10. Why are proprietorships more common than partnerships?

ANALYZE INFORMATION

1. Assume you are planning to open a business of your own by using your home computer to prepare designs and slogans that can be printed and ironed on T-shirts. You already have the computer but need a few other items. However, you are not sure you really want to start such a business. To help you decide, make two columns on a sheet of paper or your word processor: Why I *Would* Like Running My Own Business and Why I *Would Not* Like Running My Own Business. Fill in all your reasons. When you finish, study the two lists and write a paragraph indicating whether you have the essential characteristics of a successful business owner.

2. Alvares invested $80,000 and Navarro invested $60,000 in their partnership business. They share profits and losses in proportion to their investments. What amount should each receive of the $33,600 profit earned last year?

3. Feng and Cooke had invested equal amounts in a partnership business. Later the business failed with $40,000 in liabilities (debts) and only $15,000 in assets (property). In addition to a share of the assets of the business, Cooke had $35,000 of other personal property at the time of the failure, but Feng had only $5,000 of additional personal property. Other than the partnership property, what amount will be required of each partner to pay the debts of the partnership? What would happen if Feng could not pay his or her share?

4. Lamar Johnson plans to go into business for himself. He wants to own a men's clothing store. He believes that he has adequate experience in this area, having managed a clothing department in a large local department store for several years. Lamar thinks that he has sufficient capital, but it may be a little tight financially getting through the first year of operation.

Katasha Thomas, a long-time friend of Lamar's, is also planning to open a business. Her women's clothing store will be located next to Lamar's in the same busy shopping area. Although Katasha has almost no experience in the clothing business, she did work part-time one summer in a fashion shop. And now she has a degree in finance from the local university. Her uncle is willing to lend her the money needed to start the business.

Both Katasha and Lamar have discussed their plans. The idea of forming a partnership has been mentioned, but they are not quite sure what to do. Form a committee of three to five students in order to (a) discuss the situation and then (b) prepare a summary of your committee's recommendations to the two people involved.

5. Assume that the balance sheet of the partnership of Tran and Nizami at the time they closed the business appeared as follows:

Assets

Cash	$18,000
Merchandise	40,000
Fixtures and Equipment	24,000
Land and Building	108,000
Total	$190,000

Claims Against Assets

Accounts Payable (Liabilities)	$10,000
N. S. Tran, Capital	90,000
A. J. Nizami, Capital	90,000
Total	$190,000

When selling the assets, the partners sold the merchandise for $32,000, the fixtures and equipment for $18,000, and the land and building for $110,000. After paying their debts, what amount of the remaining cash should each partner receive?

6. Assume you are considering forming a small business in your state. Search for information that will help you decide whether to open a sole proprietorship or a partnership. Use your school or public library to obtain information for writing a report on business plans, legal advice, and general state assistance. If you have access to the Internet, you can find information from a government Web site, such as the Small Business Administration (www.sba.gov), or from a magazine targeted to small businesses, such as www. blackenterprise.com, www.incmag.com, or www.entrepreneurmag. com. You could also try search engines such as www. askjeeves.com and www.alltheweb.com.

SOLVE BUSINESS PROBLEMS

CASE 5-1

Sharon Gillespie, John Jensen, and Laura Cho have been close friends for years. About two years ago they formed a partnership that builds Web pages for small entrepreneurs who want to expand their businesses. Sharon, John, and Laura are experts at what they do. However, their partnership has not been very successful and is not growing. John is in charge of finding and dealing with customers and handling necessary paperwork tasks. Both Sharon and Laura build the Web pages for their customers.

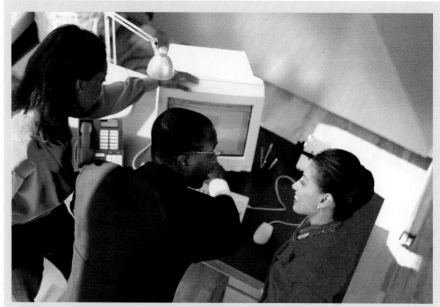

Recently, John confided to Laura that he is getting many complaints about Sharon's treatment of customers. "That may be the major reason why we aren't doing that well, but what can we do about it?" He continued, "Her customers don't often come back to us when they need to add new products or offer new services on their Web pages. Some have even jotted complaints about her on the bills I send them. Yesterday one customer said he'll take his business elsewhere if we don't replace her." The phone rang, and John excused himself to answer it.

After thinking about this for a while, Laura told John, "We have to get rid of her because she isn't going to change. If we want our business to survive and grow, let's ask her to leave. What else can we do?"

John paused and then said, "She owns one-third of our business. You can't fire a partner."

Laura asked, "Didn't our lawyer provide for this type of problem in our partnership agreement? Or maybe it's in our business plan."

"No, it's not in either place," John responded. "We have to work this out together."

Think Critically:

Your instructor may wish to place you into groups of three students each to answer the following questions and for each group to report their answers to the class.

1. What conditions existed before the partnership was formed that gave rise to this problem?
2. How important are the skills and personalities of the partners when considering the formation of a partnership?
3. Can Sharon's attitude toward customers somehow be changed? If yes, how?

4. What is the best solution for solving this problem? Carefully explain your answer.
5. Do you believe that John and Sharon would be better off trading jobs with each other?
6. How is this case situation different from that of student groups that attempt to solve other types of group problems?

CASE 5-2

John Willis, who is 27 and single, had just completed his fifth year of employment as a carpenter for a very small homebuilder. His boss, the sole owner of the company, is Tyrone Young. A few days ago, Tyrone asked John if he would like to become a partner, which he could do by contributing $70,000. In turn, John would receive 40 percent of all profits earned by the business. John had saved $30,000 and could borrow the balance needed from his grandmother at a low interest rate, but he would have to pay her back within 15 years.

John was undecided about becoming a partner. He liked the idea but he also knew there were risks and concerns. To help him make up his mind, he decided to talk to Tyrone at lunch. Here is how the conversation went.

John: *I've been giving your offer a lot of thought, Tyrone. It's a tough decision, and I don't want to make the wrong one. So I'd like to chat with you about some of the problems involved in running a business.*

Tyrone: *Sure. I struggled with these issues about 15 years ago. When you own your own business, you're the boss. No one can tell you what to do or push you around. You can set up your own hours and make all the decisions. I enjoy the feeling of ownership.*

John: *I don't know if I'm ready to become part owner of a business. I'm still young and single, and I like working for you. I'm not sure I want all those responsibilities—getting customers, paying bills, and buying tools and lumber. You say you set your own hours, but I know you're already working when I arrive each morning, and you're still here when I leave in the evening. I know you spend some nights in the office, because I see the lights on when I drive by.*

Tyrone: *Well, I do put in many hours. That goes with the territory. But I don't mind all those hours because I like making decisions. And, when you join me as a partner, we'll share the work.*

John: *Then I'll be working longer hours. Both of us could go to work for that big new contracting firm on the other side of town. They could struggle with all the problems and decisions. Then we could work shorter hours and have more time to relax.*

Think Critically:

1. Do you think John is seriously ready to become a partner? Explain your answer.
2. If you were in John's position, how would you decide? Explain.
3. If John decides to accept Tyrone's offer, what action should be taken?
4. Find information from the library or Internet that might help John make a decision. One possible source is the Web site www.sba. gov/starting/indexstartup.html.

PROJECT: MY BUSINESS, INC.

New owners often start a business without carefully considering other possible forms of ownership. In this chapter, you will evaluate the advantages and disadvantages of the proprietorship and partnership forms of ownership for your new business.

DATA COLLECTION

1. Review copies of magazines written for entrepreneurs. Identify the current issues and problems faced by individual business own-

ers as well as the successful operating procedures described in the magazines.

2. Identify a person who currently is or has been a partner in a business. Ask the person to identify the advantages and disadvantages of operating a business as a partnership from his or her viewpoint.

3. Using the Internet, if possible, find a sample copy or an outline of a business plan. Speak with a banker or your business mentor about the importance of business plans for new businesses. Ask that person to describe the elements he or she feels are most important in a good business plan.

ANALYSIS

1. You have found a partner who wants to invest $6,000 and become involved in the operation of the business. You have already invested $12,000. Develop a simple partnership agreement for the business. After you have completed the agreement, ask your business mentor to review it with you.

2. Develop a chart that compares the proprietorship and partnership forms of business ownership for your business. Be certain to consider financial, personal, and management factors. When you have finished the analysis, decide whether you will remain a sole proprietor or form a partnership.

3. Develop an outline for a business plan for your new business. Begin to list the information that will go into each section of the plan. Identify the information you need to complete the business plan and the sources of that information. Continue to develop the business plan during the time you are working on this continuing project.

CORPORATE FORMS OF BUSINESS OWNERSHIP

OBJECTIVES

6-1 Explain the basic features of a corporation.

6-2 Describe how a corporation is formed and organized.

6-3 List some of the major advantages and disadvantages of the corporate form of business.

6-4 Describe several specialized forms of business organizations.

CORPORATE CONCEPT

hanh Vu came to this country from Vietnam ten years ago and earned a college business degree. After graduation he worked as a manager in a small firm, where he learned a great deal. But after five years, the job became less challenging. He wondered about opening his own business with the money he had saved, but that seemed too risky.

Surely there was some way to be an entrepreneur without having to assume so much responsibility alone or with a partner. The partnership idea sounded acceptable, but fear of lawsuits from creditors if he didn't do well haunted him. Yet his fear of unlimited liability did not stop him from thinking about starting a business.

On his way home from work one day, Thanh stopped to get his hair styled. He overheard two other customers talking about changing their small partnership to a corporation. One said, "We would pay higher taxes." The other responded, "But our financial liability would be less than in

our partnership." Thanh listened intently but said nothing until after the first person replied, "But we can't expand our successful business unless we can raise more money."

By now Thanh could no longer restrain himself. "Excuse me for listening, but I have an idea. I'm a manager and have a degree in business; but more important, I'm looking for an opportunity to become a business owner." The two men looked at each other and nodded. "Let's hear your idea," one said cautiously.

"There's a special type of corporation that permits you to be a corporation but allows you to pay taxes as if you were still a partnership," Thanh replied. "And if you're looking for another stockholder who can invest some money and help expand the business, I'd be very interested in talking with you."

After the introductions and handshakes, they scheduled a luncheon meeting for the next day.

In Chapter 5 you learned about proprietorships and partnerships as legal forms of organizing a business. This chapter will deal with the features and formation of corporations. In addition, you will learn about special organizational structures: limited liability companies, joint ventures, virtual corporations, nonprofit corporations, and cooperatives. If you were to join the three people in the opening story at their luncheon meeting tomorrow, you would need to understand the contents of this chapter.

■ CORPORATIONS

Corporations are towers on the business landscape. While proprietorships are many in number, they are generally small in size. In comparison, corporations are few in number, but generally large in size. Because corporations tend to be large, they play a powerful role in this country and in others. For example, corporations employ millions of people and provide consumers with many of the goods and services they need and want. In a recent year, corporate sales of goods and services were over 17 times more than sales from proprietorships, and over 16 times more than sales from partnerships in the United States.

Not all corporations are large. While corporations such as Ford, Compaq, and K-Mart are known to almost everyone, many small corporations also exist. Small corporations are popular for reasons you will discover later in this chapter.

Because the corporation plays a vital role in business, we need to understand its basic features as well as its advantages and disadvantages. To gain knowledge of the basic features of the corporation, we can follow York, Burton, and Chan as they consider incorporating their fast-growing food store partnership, which they launched in the last chapter.

■ BASIC FEATURES

Elena Morales, a lawyer, helped York, Burton, and Chan prepare the partnership agreement under which they now operate. The partners asked Elena to describe a corporation to them. She stated that a **corporation** is a business owned by a group of people and authorized by the state in which it is located to act as though it were a single person, separate from its owners. To get permission to form a corporation, organizers must obtain a charter. A **charter** (often called a **certificate of incorporation**) is the official document through which a state grants the power to operate as a corporation.

A corporation is, in a sense, an artificial person created by the laws of the state. A corporation can make contracts, borrow money, own property, and sue or be sued in its own name. Any act performed for the corporation by an authorized person, such as an employee, is done in the name of the business. For example, the treasurer of a corporation has the power to borrow money for the business. An unauthorized employee, such as a receptionist who was hired to answer the phone and greet visitors, could not borrow money for the corporation.

Morales further explained the important parts played by three key types of people in corporations: (1) stockholders, (2) directors, and (3) officers.

STOCKHOLDERS   **Stockholders** (often called **shareholders**) are the owners of a corporation. Ownership is divided into equal parts called **shares.** A person who buys one share becomes a stockholder. Therefore, thousands of people can own a corporation. Each stockholder receives a certificate from the corporation, which shows the number of shares owned. Stockholders have a number of basic rights, including the following:

1. To transfer ownership to others.

2. To vote for members of the ruling body of the corporation and other special matters that may be brought before the stockholders.

3. To receive dividends. **Dividends** are profits that are distributed to stockholders on a per-share basis. The decision to distribute profits is made by the ruling body of the corporation.

4. To buy new shares of stock in proportion to one's present investment should the corporation issue more shares.

5. To share in the net proceeds (cash received from the sale of all assets less the payment of all debts) should the corporation go out of business.

A stockholder does not have the same financial responsibility as a partner; that is, there is no liability beyond the extent of the stockholder's ownership. If the corporation fails, a stockholder can lose only the money invested. Creditors cannot collect anything further from the stockholder.

DIRECTORS The **board of directors** (often shortened to **directors** or the **board**) is the ruling body of the corporation. Board members are elected by the stockholders. Directors develop plans and policies to guide the corporation as well as appoint officers to carry out the plans. If the corporation is performing successfully, its board is content to deal with policy issues and review the progress of the company. However, if the corporation's profits fall, or if it experiences other serious difficulties, the board often steps in and takes an active role in the operation of the business.

In large firms, boards generally consist of 10 to 25 directors. A few board members are top executives from within the corporation. The directors often are from outside the corporation and are usually executives from other businesses or people from nonprofit organizations, such as college professors. Often, directors are stockholders who hold many shares. But directors need not be stockholders. People who hold few or no shares are sometimes elected to the board because they have valuable knowledge needed by the board to make sound decisions. In some countries, such as Sweden, France, and China, an employee of the company is also a board member.

Business experts believe that in the 21st century, corporate boards will need to have one or more directors with expertise in the following areas: telecommunications and technology; marketing; international markets; top-level finance; restructuring; entrepreneurial skills; and service industries.

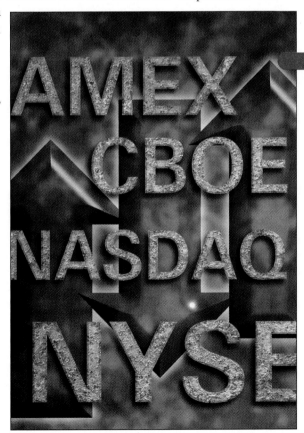

ILLUSTRATION 6-1

A person can become a stockholder in any one of hundreds of major corporations. In which corporations would you be interested in owning stock?

ETHICAL ISSUES

TROUBLE IN THE BOARDROOM

Experts agree that top management greatly influences the extent to which ethics are practiced in corporations by CEOs and boards of directors. Shareholders assume that their elected directors are ethical, but are they?

The relationships between shareholders, boards, and CEOs should be as harmonious as possible. In practice, however, CEOs sometimes manipulate boards. As a result, employees, retirees, customers, and shareholders often suffer.

For example, CEOs know that the boards who hire them can also fire them. As a result, CEOs want to build relationships with board members. CEOs in firms that are not doing well are often motivated to take defensive action. One such defense is to get elected as chairperson of the board. In this way, CEOs set meeting agendas and thereby control topics that are discussed. CEOs can also recommend friends as nominees to the board for stockholders to elect via proxy statements. Through such actions, CEOs build loyal followers.

On the other hand, directors who are elected by shareholders and who are loyal to CEOs may be disloyal to the stockholders they represent. A condition like this creates problems.

For example, CEO salaries may be raised despite poor performance. A CEO's plans may be approved without adequate review. During tough competitive periods when a firm has difficulty making a profit, everyone is hurt. That's when employees get fired and stockholders lose money.

Employees get hurt in another way when employee pension funds are invested in corporations by the fund managers. Pension funds are pools of money set aside for employee retirement benefits. When corporations do poorly, managers of large pension funds try to see that changes are made within these companies. Changes made in recent years as the result of action taken by pension fund managers include these examples. First, boards now select more directors from outside firms who are more critical of poor CEO leadership. Second, more boards take greater care in selecting, evaluating, and paying CEOs.

Ethics in boardrooms have been improving gradually. Now good boards listen to stockholders and no longer permit CEOs to control them. Rather, good boards control CEOs. And good CEOs encourage frank discussions with their boards and stakeholders.

THINK CRITICALLY

1. What defensive actions have CEOs taken that might cause boards of directors to perform their jobs improperly?
2. What happens when boards and CEOs do not adequately represent stockholders?
3. Do you believe the ethics of corporations differ much from the ethics in nonprofit organizations, such as between the superintendent of a school system and the board of education? Explain your answer.
4. Using a library or the Internet, find a recent report that deals with a CEO being fired by a board. Determine the causes for dismissal.

■ OFFICERS

The **officers** of a corporation are the top executives who are hired to manage the business. The board of directors appoints them. The officers of a small corporation often consist of a president, a secretary, and a treasurer. In addition, large corporations may have vice presidents in charge of major areas, such as marketing, finance, and manufacturing. The titles of these officers are often shortened to letters. For example, the top officer is called a CEO (chief executive officer) and the head financial officer is the CFO (chief financial officer).

■ FORMATION OF CORPORATIONS

Over several months, York, Burton, and Chan asked their attorney, Elena Morales, many questions. Only after careful thought did the partners decide to form a corporation. Morales told them that there were basically three steps involved. First, a series of decisions had to be made about how the corporation would be organized. Second, the proper legal forms had to be prepared and sent to the state office that handles such matters. And third, the state would review the incorporation papers and issue a charter if it approved.

PREPARING THE CERTIFICATE OF INCORPORATION Each state has its own laws for forming corporations. No federal law exists. To incorporate a business, it is necessary in most states to file a certificate of incorporation with the appropriate state office. Morales prepared the certificate of incorporation for York, Burton, and Chan shown in Figure 6-1.

Notice the general type of information called for in the certificate of incorporation. In addition to the firm name, purpose, and capital stock, it requires information about the organizers.

Naming the Business. A business is usually required by law to have a name that indicates clearly that a corporation has been formed. Words or abbreviations such as *Corporation, Corp., Incorporated,* or *Inc.* are used; see Figure 6-2 for examples. The organizers have decided to name their corporation York, Burton, and Chan, Inc.

Stating the Purpose of the Business. A certificate of incorporation requires a corporation to describe its purpose clearly. In Figure 6-1, Article 3 precisely states the purpose of the corporation: "to operate a retail food business." It allows the corporation to expand into new food lines, but it does not allow the corporation to start non-food operations. For major changes in purpose, a new request must be submitted and approved by the state.

Investing in the Business. The certificate of incorporation could not be completed until York, Burton, and Chan decided how to invest their partnership holdings in the corporation. They agreed that the assets and

FIGURE 6-1

A certificate of incorporation includes information about the organizers of a corporation.

Certificate of Incorporation of
York, Burton, and Chan, Inc.

Pursuant to Article Two of the Stock Corporation Law.

State of New York
County of Cattaraugus } ss.

We, the undersigned, for the purpose of forming a Corporation pursuant to Article Two of the Stock Corporation Law of the State of New York, do hereby make, subscribe, acknowledge and file this certificate for that purpose as follows:

We, the undersigned, do hereby Certify

First.—That all the undersigned are full age, and . . . . all . . . . are citizens of the United States, and . . . . all . . . . residents of the State of New York.

Second.—That the name of said corporation is York, Burton, and Chan, Inc.

Third.—That the purpose for which said corporation is formed is to operate a retail food business.

Fourth.—That the amount of the Capital Stock of the said corporation is . . . . One Million . . . . Dollars . ($ . . . 1,000,000 . . .) . . . . to consist of . . Ten Thousand . . . (10,000) . . . shares of the par value of . . . . One Hundred . . . . dollars ($ . . . . . 100 . . . . . .) each.

Fifth.—That the office of said corporation is to be located in the . . City . . . . of Buffalo . . . . , County of . . . . . Cattaraugus . . . . and State of New York.

Sixth.—That the duration of said corporation is to be . . . perpetual . . . .

Seventh.—That the number of Directors of said corporation is . . . three . . . .

Eighth.—That the names and post office addresses of the Directors until the first annual meeting are as follows:

Jennifer L. York . . 1868 Buffalo Street, Buffalo, NY 14760-1436 . . . .
Robert R. Burton . 1309 Main Street, Buffalo, NY 14760-1436 . . . .
Lu Chan . . . . 4565 Erie Avenue, Niagara Falls, NY 14721-2348

Ninth.—That the names and post office addresses of the subscribers and the number of shares of stock which each agrees to take in said corporation are as follows:

Names	Post Office Addresses	No. of Shares
Jennifer L. York	1868 Buffalo Street	
	Buffalo, NY 14760-1436	2,217
Robert R. Burton	1309 Main Street	
	Buffalo, NY 14760-1436	2,217
Lu Chan	4565 Erie Avenue	
	Niagara Falls, NY 14721-2348	2,217

Tenth.—That the meetings of the Board of Directors shall be held only within the State of New York . . . . at Buffalo . . . .

In Witness Whereof, we have made, subscribed, and executed this certificate . . . in duplicate . . . . the . . . . tenth . . . . . day of . . . . September . . . in the year . . . . Two thousand . . . .

Jennifer L. York
Robert R. Burton
Lu Chan

debts of the partnership should be taken over by the corporation. They further agreed that their capital (net worth or *equity*) of $221,700 each should be invested in the corporation. **Capital stock** (or simply **stock**) is the general term applied to the shares of ownership of a corporation.

Here is how the details were worked out. The organizers requested authorization from the state to issue $1,000,000 in capital stock, as shown in Figure 6-1. Shares were valued at $100 each at the time of incorporation. There were 10,000 shares in all ($1,000,000 divided by $100 equals 10,000). York, Burton, and Chan each agreed to purchase 2,217 shares, as shown in Figure 6-3.

The 3,349 unissued shares (the difference between the 10,000 authorized shares and the 6,651 shares bought by the organizers) can be sold at a later date to raise more funds to expand the business.

Paying Incorporation Costs. Usually a new corporation must pay an organization tax, based on the amount of its capital stock. In addition, a new corporation usually pays a filing fee before the state will issue a charter entitling the business to operate as a corporation. In some states, the existence of the corporation begins when the application or certificate of incorporation has been filed with the Department of State.

OPERATING THE NEW CORPORATION   York, Burton, and Chan, Inc., received approval to operate as a corporation. They turned their attention next to getting the business started.

Getting Organized. One of the first steps in getting the new corporation underway is to prepare a balance sheet or statement of financial position. The new corporation's balance sheet is shown in Figure 6-4.

The ownership of the corporation is in the same hands as was the ownership of the partnership. The ownership of the corporation, however, is evidenced by the issued capital stock. The former partners have each received a stock certificate indicating that each owns 2,217 shares of stock with a value of $100 a share.

York	2,217 shares x $100 per share =	$221,700
Burton	2,217 shares x $100 per share =	$221,700
Chan	2,217 shares x $100 per share =	$221,700
Total		$665,100

ASSETS			CLAIMS AGAINST ASSETS	
Cash	$ 240,000		Accounts Payable (Liabilities)	$ 74,900
Merchandise	60,000		Capital Stock	665,100
Equipment	90,000			
Land & Buildings	350,000			
Total	$740,000		Total	$740,000

FIGURE 6-4

Balance sheet of York, Burton, and Chan, Inc.

The three stockholders own the business and elect themselves directors. The new directors select officers. York is appointed president; Burton, vice president; and Chan, secretary and treasurer. An organization chart of the new corporation is shown in Figure 6-5.

Handling Voting Rights. The owners agreed that each owner will have 2,217 votes on matters arising in the meetings of the stockholders. Voting stockholders usually have one vote for each share owned. However, if Chan, for instance, sold 1,200 of his shares to Burton, Burton would own 3,417 shares, or more than 50 percent of the total 6,651 shares of stock that have been issued. Then Burton could control the corporation; that is, York and Chan would lose if Burton voted differently from them on an important issue. Burton would have more votes than York and Chan together.

Their lawyer told the officers of the corporation that they must send each stockholder notices of all stockholders' meetings to be held. Even stockholders with just one share must receive notices of meetings. If stockholders cannot attend the meetings personally, they can be represented through a proxy that can be submitted by Internet, phone, or mail. A **proxy** is a written authorization for someone to vote on behalf of the person signing the proxy. It is common practice for a proxy form to be enclosed with the letter that announces a stockholders' meeting. One example of a proxy that a corporation might use is shown in Figure 6-6.

■ CLOSE AND OPEN CORPORATIONS

A **close corporation** (also called a **closely held corporation**) is one that does not offer its shares of stock for public sale. Just a few stockholders own it; some of them may help run the business in the same manner as partners operate a business. York, Burton, and Chan, Inc., is an example of a close corporation. The three former partners own all the stock and operate the business as well.

In most states, a close corporation does not need to make its financial activities known to the public. Its stock is not offered for general sale. It must, however, prepare reports for the state from which it obtained its

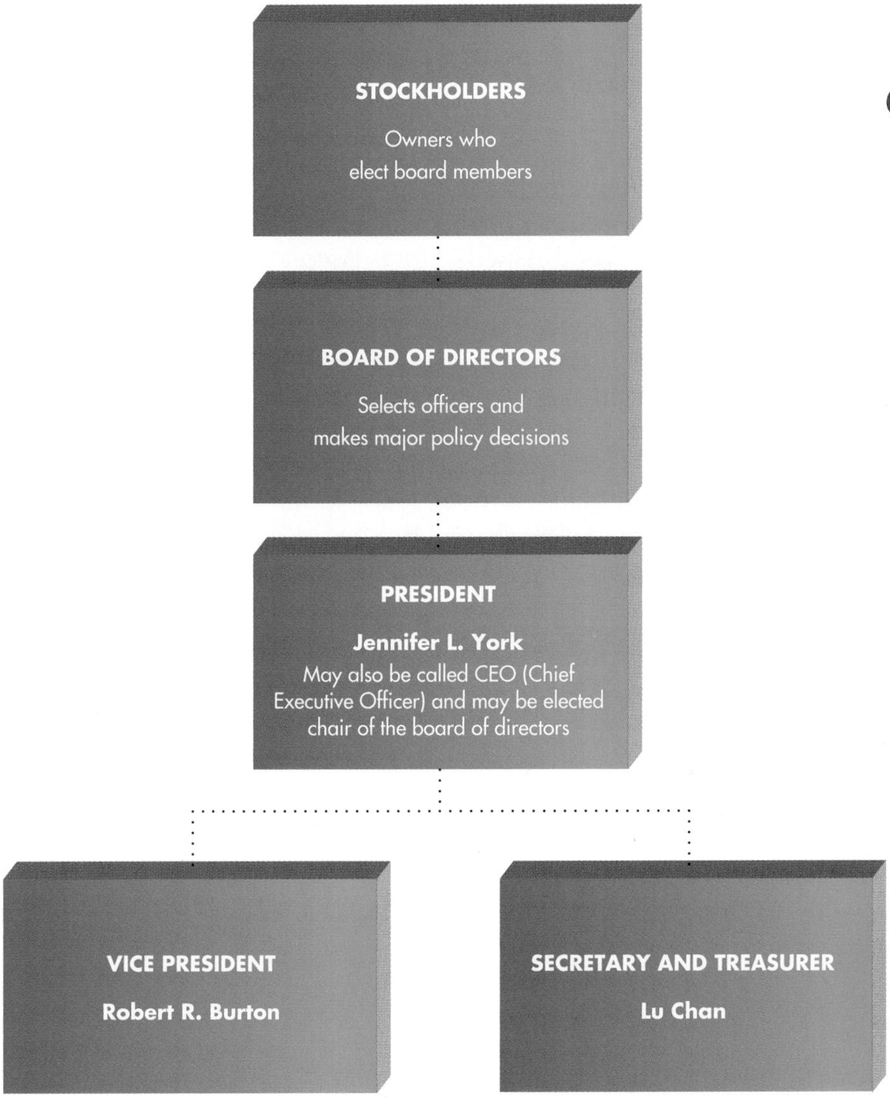

STOCKHOLDERS

Owners who
elect board members

BOARD OF DIRECTORS

Selects officers and
makes major policy decisions

PRESIDENT

Jennifer L. York

May also be called CEO (Chief
Executive Officer) and may be elected
chair of the board of directors

VICE PRESIDENT

Robert R. Burton

SECRETARY AND TREASURER

Lu Chan

FIGURE 6-5

An organization chart of a corporation.

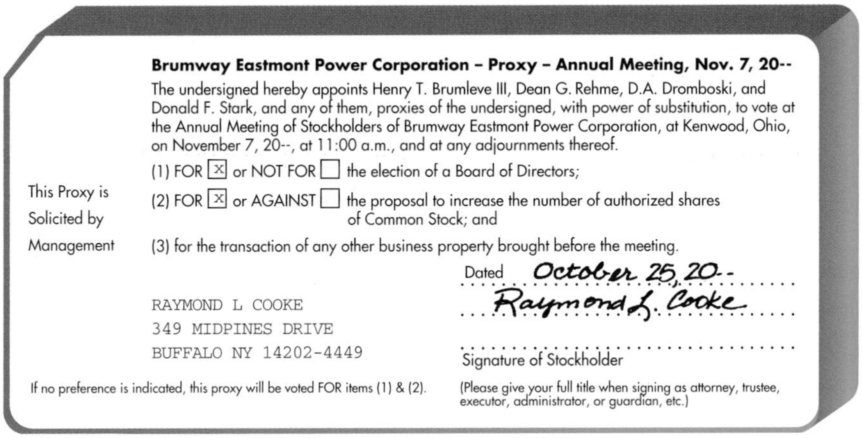

Brumway Eastmont Power Corporation – Proxy – Annual Meeting, Nov. 7, 20--

The undersigned hereby appoints Henry T. Brumleve III, Dean G. Rehme, D.A. Dromboski, and Donald F. Stark, and any of them, proxies of the undersigned, with power of substitution, to vote at the Annual Meeting of Stockholders of Brumway Eastmont Power Corporation, at Kenwood, Ohio, on November 7, 20--, at 11:00 a.m., and at any adjournments thereof.

(1) FOR ☒ or NOT FOR ☐ the election of a Board of Directors;

This Proxy is
Solicited by
Management

(2) FOR ☒ or AGAINST ☐ the proposal to increase the number of authorized shares of Common Stock; and

(3) for the transaction of any other business property brought before the meeting.

Dated   *October 25, 20--*

Raymond L. Cooke

RAYMOND L COOKE
349 MIDPINES DRIVE
BUFFALO NY 14202-4449

Signature of Stockholder

If no preference is indicated, this proxy will be voted FOR items (1) & (2).

(Please give your full title when signing as attorney, trustee, executor, administrator, or guardian, etc.)

FIGURE 6-6

A proxy signed by a stockholder.

charter. And it must, for tax purposes, prepare reports for all states in which it operates.

An **open corporation** (also called a **publicly owned corporation**) is one that offers its shares of stock for public sale. Figure 6-7 shows a newspaper ad announcing the sale of common stock to the public. A corporation must file a registration statement with the Securities and Exchange Commission (SEC) containing extensive details about the corporation and the proposed issue of stock. A condensed version of this registration statement, called a prospectus, must be furnished to each prospective buyer of newly offered stocks (or bonds). A **prospectus** is a formal summary of the chief features of the business and its stock offering. Prospective buyers can find information in the prospectus that will help them decide whether or not to buy stock in the corporation.

Open corporations often have a large number of stockholders, perhaps hundreds of thousands or more. Many of the stockholders in large corporations own only a few shares. But because of the great number of stockholders, such a corporation has a large amount of capital. When

FIGURE 6-7

An open corporation must offer its shares for sale to the public.

This announcement is neither an offer to sell nor a solicitation of an offer to buy any of these Securities. The offer is made only by the Prospectus.

2,530,000 Shares

GALACTICA, INC.

Common Stock

. . . .
Price $18 a Share
. . . .

Copies of the Prospectus may be obtained in any State from only such of the undersigned as may legally offer these Securities in compliance with the securities laws of such State.

Morgan Stanley & Co.	Hambrecht & Quist
Incorporated	Incorporated
Goldman, Sachs & Co.	Cowen & Company
Donaldson, Lufkin & Jenrette	Kidder, Peabody & Co.
Securities Corporation	Incorporated
Merrill Lynch & Co.	Montgomery Securities

people buy stock, they are investing their capital (money) in the corporation. If the corporation fares well, stockholders will earn a return on their investment by receiving dividends and by selling their stock for more than they paid for it. If the corporation does not do well, stockholders may receive no dividends and may even have to sell their stock for less than they paid for it. If the corporation goes out of business, stockholders may lose their entire investment.

■ ADVANTAGES OF CORPORATIONS

The corporation has a number of advantages as compared with the proprietorship and partnership. Four such advantages are discussed below.

AVAILABLE SOURCES OF CAPITAL   The corporation can obtain money from several sources. One of those sources is the sale of shares to stockholders. This special privilege helps to raise enough capital for running large-scale businesses. Because corporations are regulated closely, people usually invest more willingly than in proprietorships and partnerships. Also, corporations usually find borrowing large sums of money less of a problem than do proprietorships or partnerships.

LIMITED LIABILITY OF STOCKHOLDERS   Except in a few situations, the owners (stockholders) are not legally liable for the debts of the corporation beyond their investments in the shares purchased. Thus, people—whether they have only a few dollars to invest or thousands of dollars—can invest in a corporation without the possibility of incurring a liability beyond their original investment.

PERMANENCY OF EXISTENCE   The corporation is a more permanent type of organization than the proprietorship or the partnership. It can continue to operate indefinitely, or only as long as the term stated in the charter. The death or withdrawal of an owner (stockholder) does not affect its life.

EASE IN TRANSFERRING OWNERSHIP   It is easy to transfer ownership in a corporation. A stockholder may sell stock to another person and transfer the stock certificate, which represents ownership, to the new owner. When shares are transferred, the transfer of ownership is indicated in the records of the corporation. A new certificate is issued in the name of the new stockholder. Millions of shares are bought and sold every day.

■ DISADVANTAGES OF CORPORATIONS

Although there are several distinct advantages to the corporation, there are also disadvantages. A discussion of some of the major disadvantages follows.

TAXATION   The corporation is usually subject to more taxes than are imposed on the proprietorship and the partnership. Some taxes that are unique to the corporation are a filing fee, which is payable on application for a charter; an organization tax, which is based on the amount of authorized capital stock; an annual state tax, based on the profits; and a federal income tax.

Another tax disadvantage for corporations is that profits distributed to stockholders as dividends are taxed twice. This double taxation occurs in two steps. The corporation first pays taxes on its profits as just described. Then it distributes some of these profits to shareholders as dividends, and the shareholders pay taxes on the dividends they receive. Most other industrialized countries do not permit double taxation on corporate profits. (Small close corporations with few stockholders may avoid double taxation by changing their form of ownership, which you will learn about later in this chapter.)

GOVERNMENT REGULATIONS AND REPORTS   A corporation cannot do business wherever it pleases. To form a corporation, an application for a charter must be submitted to the appropriate state official, usually the secretary of state. York, Burton, and Chan, Inc., has permission to conduct business only in the state of New York. Should it wish to conduct business in other states, each state will probably require the corporation to obtain a license and pay a fee to do business in that state. State incorporation fees are not very expensive. The attorney's fee accounts for the major costs of incorporating. Each state has different laws that govern the formation of corporations.

The regulation of corporations by states and by the federal government is extensive. A corporation must file special reports to the state from which it received its charter as well as in other states where it conducts business. The federal government requires firms whose stock is publicly traded to publish financial data. As a result, an increased need arises for detailed financial records and reports.

STOCKHOLDERS' RECORDS Corporations that have many stockholders have added problems—and expenses—in communicating with stockholders and in handling stockholders' records. By law, stockholders must be informed of corporate matters, notified of meetings, and given the right to vote on important matters. Letters and reports must be sent to stockholders on a regular basis. In addition, each time a share of stock is bought or sold and whenever a dividend is paid, detailed records must be kept. Keeping records for the thousands of stockholders of General Electric, for example, is a time-consuming and costly task.

CHARTER RESTRICTIONS A corporation is allowed to engage only in those activities that are stated in its charter. Should York, Burton, and Chan, Inc., wish to sell hardware, the organizers would have to go to the state to obtain a new charter or change the old one. As a partnership, they could have added the other line of merchandise without government approval.

■ BUSINESSES SUITED TO BEING CORPORATIONS

Even though the corporation has major disadvantages, a survey of business firms shows that almost every kind of business exists as a corporation, including Web-based firms. The corporate form of ownership is especially suited to the following types of businesses:

1. Businesses that require large amounts of capital, such as airlines and auto manufacturers. To start a 500-room hotel, for example, requires millions of dollars for buying land and for constructing and furnishing the hotel.
2. Businesses that may have uncertain futures, such as amusement parks, publishers of new magazines, and makers of novelty goods. The publisher of a new magazine, for example, takes a great risk in assuming that the magazine will be popular enough to make a profit. Organizers of firms with uncertain futures do not wish to assume the added financial risks that fall upon a proprietor or a partner in case the business fails.

Each form of business organization has special advantages to owners of different types of businesses. While the corporate form of organization is suited to firms that have uncertain futures or that require large amounts of capital, the partnership is especially suited to small, growing business firms. The proprietorship, in comparison, has great appeal to the person who wants to run a small business.

ILLUSTRATION 6-3
Why would the corporate form of ownership be suited to a mining company?

Joint ventures often include business partners from foreign countries. For example, Ford Motor Company produces cars in a joint venture with Mazda. Some multinational corporations have formed joint ventures with companies in once-communist countries. This helps the corporations expand into new markets. At the same time, the joint ventures serve as a way to help companies in the previously communist nations to learn about doing business in a free market economy.

■ SPECIALIZED TYPES OF ORGANIZATIONS

In addition to sole proprietorships, partnerships, and corporations, organizations can be legally formed as joint ventures, virtual corporations, limited liability companies, nonprofit corporations, and cooperatives.

■ JOINT VENTURES

At times businesses want to join forces in order to achieve an important objective. A **joint venture** is an agreement among two or more businesses to work together to provide a good or service. The legal formation of the business is not important. For example, a sole proprietorship and a corporation could agree to work together. Each partner in the joint venture is expected to bring management expertise and/or money to the venture. Many major corporations today have learned that alone they may not have all the expertise or capital needed.

An example of a joint venture might include an agreement between two major contractors to connect two cities by building a tunnel for cars under a river. A company working alone may not have the capital to build the tunnel, and each may lack special equipment or skills that the other firm has. By forming a joint venture, they can acquire the expertise to build the tunnel that they could not complete alone. There are thousands of joint ventures between and among many companies. Many Web-based companies rely extensively on joint ventures to build their businesses.

Because organizations must adapt quickly to compete effectively, a more fluid form of the joint venture, the virtual corporation, is evolving in the world of business. The **virtual corporation** is a network of companies that form alliances among themselves as needed to take advantage of fast-changing market conditions. Puma, the athletic shoe company, for example, is a virtual corporation. Puma markets its shoes in Germany. A small network of Asian companies purchases the materials to make the shoes. Other companies in China, Taiwan, Indonesia, and Korea manufacture the shoes. Then separate companies on all continents sell the shoes. In all, 80 companies worldwide participate in making and selling Puma shoes.

Virtual corporations tend to be more temporary relationships than are joint ventures. Several companies within the network may team up to take advantage of a market opportunity. These same companies may also work with a different combination of partners within the network, depending on the expertise needed to take advantage of a particular market opportunity at that time.

An example of a virtual corporation might include the following situation. Company A wishes to rush to market a new sophisticated computer but needs special parts that it does not produce. Company A learns that Company B produces one part and Company C produces the other needed part. Unfortunately, none of the three companies has customers who would likely have an interest in the new computer. After searching, the firms find that Company D sells computers to customers with special needs. Ultimately, all three companies agree to join with Company A to market the new computer. This virtual corporation situation, which is illustrated in Figure 6-8, makes it possible for all four companies to benefit when no one company could have made and marketed the new computer quickly on its own. Many companies involved in selling the goods of other firms, especially Web-based firms, are virtual corporations.

CYBER COMMUNICATION

Business memos are informal messages sent to persons within an organization. Sending a memo is a quick, easy way to communicate with a colleague or manager within your own department, in another department, or in another company office. The memo is a streamlined, efficient way to send a message to an internal audience.

In many businesses today, e-mail has taken over formal memo writing. E-mail memos are composed, transmitted, and usually read on a computer screen. They can be sent to more than one receiver; they take less time to format and key than letters; and they are less complex and time-consuming than meetings or conference calls.

Before you can organize an effective e-mail message, you must first plan your message. This requires asking yourself four questions: (1) What do I hope to accomplish in sending this message? (2) What do I want the receiver to do or to understand? (3) What does the receiver need to know about the main idea in order to respond to or understand the message? (4) What do I want the receiver to gain from the message?

ACTIVITY Assume that one of your classmates was out sick today. You have volunteered to send the classmate a brief memo describing what happened during the class session. Think about what you want to communicate in your message. Then write your answers to the four questions listed above.

LIMITED LIABILITY COMPANIES

Small, growing partnerships are especially attracted to the limited liability company (LLC) form of corporation, which was once called an "S-corporation." The **limited liability company (LLC)** is a special type of corporation that is taxed as if it were a sole proprietorship or

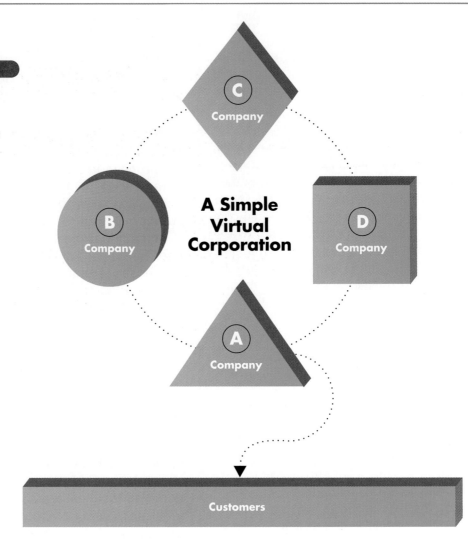

FIGURE 6-8

A virtual corporation is a network of companies that form alliances among themselves as needed to take advantage of fast-changing market conditions.

partnership. Two factors make LLCs popular. First, a major disadvantage of a partnership is unlimited liability, whereas a major advantage of a corporation is its limited liability. Second, a major advantage of a partnership is its lower income tax rate, whereas a disadvantage of a corporation is a higher income tax rate than that paid by partnerships. Stockholders also have to pay personal income taxes on dividends distributed by a corporation (double taxation). The LLC provides an ideal solution—lower taxes and limited liability. In addition, the profits from the corporation go directly to the stockholders, who then include the profits on their individual income tax returns. Double taxation is avoided. York, Burton, and Chan, Inc., would qualify for this special tax advantage. The LLC also may be the solution to the dilemma that Thanh Vu and his two acquaintances faced at the start of this chapter.

However, not all companies are eligible for LLC status. A few important rules determine eligibility. First, a firm must have no more than

35 stockholders. Second, the business cannot own 80 percent or more of the stock of another corporation. Third, not more than 25 percent of the income of the corporation can be from sources other than for the purpose(s) stated in the charter. And, fourth, all stockholders must be individuals who are permanent citizens or residents of this country. Large corporations and multinational firms do not meet these qualifications. Many partnerships, however, do qualify and find the LLC to be highly favorable.

ILLUSTRATION 6-4

Nonprofit organizations do not make a profit for distribution to stockholders. Can you name some examples of nonprofit organizations in your community?

NONPROFIT CORPORATIONS

Close and open corporations, as discussed earlier, are businesses that operate mainly to make a profit for their owners. A **nonprofit corporation,** on the other hand, is an organization that does not pay taxes and does not exist to make a profit. Organizations that manage cities or operate schools are examples of nonprofit corporations. Because a nonprofit corporation is not established as a profit-making enterprise, it does not pay dividends to shareholders. Otherwise, it operates much like a close or open corporation. The Rotary Club, private schools and universities, United Way, and most local hospitals are other examples of nonprofit organizations. Even Educational Testing Service, the company that makes the Scholastic Aptitude Test (SAT), is a nonprofit organization.

In this country, nonprofit corporations provide nearly one-third of the GDP. However, in most other countries, nonprofit corporations contribute much more to the GDP. The principles of business and management provided in this text apply equally to managers who run profit-making as well as nonprofit corporations.

QUASI-PUBLIC CORPORATIONS

A business that is important to society, but lacks the profit potential to attract private investors, is often operated by local, state, or federal government. Government financial support (called a *subsidy*) may also be required. This type of business is usually described as a **quasi-public corporation.** Government imposes regulatory controls over quasi-public corporations.

The Tennessee Valley Authority, a rural electrification program started in the 1930s by the federal government, was one of the first quasi-public corporations. The organizations that run interstate highways, such as the Massachusetts and Pennsylvania turnpike authorities, are state-owned quasi-public corporations. At the local level, examples of quasi-public organizations include water and sewer systems, parking garages, and civic and cultural facilities. The Los Angeles County Museum of Art is a government-owned cultural organization.

■ COOPERATIVES

A **cooperative** is a business owned and operated by its user-members for the purpose of supplying themselves with goods and services. The members, who are much like stockholders in a corporation with the protection of limited liability, usually join a cooperative by buying shares of stock. The members elect a board of directors, which appoints officers to run the business. Much like a corporation, a cooperative must also obtain a charter from the state in which it is organized in order to operate. Some types of cooperatives need authorization from the federal government.

The purpose of cooperatives is to provide their members with cost and profit advantages that they do not otherwise have. For example, a group of blueberry growers believes that individually they can save money and make more profit by forming a cooperative for the purpose of selling their berries. Once the business is organized and operating, the members (owners) sell their berries through the cooperative. The cooperative markets the berries. In turn, the growers earn more than if they tried to market the berries on their own. In addition, as owners they share in the profits of the business.

With almost 19 million businesses in the United States, cooperatives represent only a small percentage of all businesses. This small number, however, does not reduce their importance. Cooperatives are popular in agriculture for buying and selling crops. And many employees belong to credit unions, where they can invest and borrow money at low interest rates. Many insurance firms are formed as cooperatives. Apartment buildings are often formed as cooperatives as well.

CHAPTER CONCEPTS

■ A corporation is a form of ownership preferred by large and growing firms, but corporations are more difficult to form than are sole proprietorships or partnerships. A business must specify its purpose, identify its owners (stockholders), elect a board of directors, select officers, establish operating policies, and prepare a charter for approval by the state.

■ A chief advantage of the corporate form of business is its limited liability feature, which limits the financial losses of stockholders to no more than their investments. Also, corporations can raise more capital for growth purposes than most other forms of business ownership. Stock can be bought and sold more easily than ownership shares in partnerships. And the life of the corporation does not end when owners sell their shares.

■ The primary downside of corporations is higher tax rates. Also, stockholders must pay taxes on dividends received (double taxation). Record-keeping and government-required paperwork is usually more extensive for corporations than for proprietorships and partnerships.

■ Joint ventures are alliances formed among companies to work together to produce a product or service that neither alone could provide efficiently. A virtual corporation is a type of joint venture in which a network of companies form temporary alliances among themselves as needed to take advantage of current market conditions. Companies within the network come together in different combinations, depending on the expertise needed to take advantage of a particular market opportunity at that time.

■ The limited liability company (LLC) is a type of organization that avoids the double-taxation levied on corporations and the unlimited liability disadvantage of partnerships. Nonprofit corporations, such as charities, are organizations that do not pay taxes and do not exist to make a profit. Cooperatives, such as credit unions, are businesses owned and operated by their user-members for the purpose of supplying themselves with goods and services. Businesses that are important to society, but are government-run because they lack the profit potential to attract private investors, are quasi-public corporations. Your local waterworks is an example.

BUILD VOCABULARY POWER

Define the following terms and concepts.

1. corporation
2. charter (certificate of incorporation)
3. stockholders (shareholders)
4. shares
5. dividends
6. board of directors (directors or board)

7. officers
8. capital stock (stock)
9. proxy
10. close corporation (closely held corporation)
11. open corporation (publicly owned corporation)
12. prospectus
13. joint venture
14. virtual corporation
15. limited liability company (LLC)
16. nonprofit corporation
17. quasi-public corporation
18. cooperative

REVIEW FACTS

1. Which form of business is fewest in total number but highest in terms of total sales of goods and services?
2. What are five basic rights of stockholders?
3. How does someone become a stockholder in a corporation? A director? An officer?
4. What steps must be taken to form a corporation?
5. By what means can stockholders vote on matters affecting the corporation even when they cannot be present at meetings?
6. How does a close corporation differ from an open corporation?
7. Give four advantages of corporations.
8. Give three disadvantages of corporations.
9. Why would a business want to form a joint venture?
10. What is the purpose of cooperatives?

DISCUSS IDEAS

1. Why can a corporation be described as an artificial person?
2. Compare the financial responsibility of owners of a corporation with that of owners of a partnership.
3. Figure 6-6 shows a proxy. If the person receiving the proxy only signed the card but did not vote for or against the numbered items, would the proxy be valid?
4. In its certificate of incorporation, why would a corporation request more shares of capital stock than are needed to get started?
5. The following people own all the shares of stock in the same corporation: Brower, 100; Ramos, 70; Forcina, 30; and Stein, 10. If all have an interest in running for the board of directors, how could it be possible for someone other than the largest stockholder to get elected?
6. Under what conditions would you be able to buy stock in York, Burton, and Chan, Inc.?
7. Explain how a joint venture could be valuable in a situation in which Corporation A has expertise in one area and Corporation B has expertise in another.

8. What conditions should exist before York, Burton, and Chan, Inc., consider becoming a limited liability company (LLC)?

9. Discuss whether the Girl Scouts organization meets the qualifications for operating as a nonprofit corporation in light of the fact that it sells a large volume of cookies each year.

10. Why are cooperatives popular in agricultural regions?

ANALYZE INFORMATION

1. George Fernandez purchased stock in the Elite Manufacturing Co., Incorporated, for $76 a share. Last year he received quarterly dividends of $1, $1, $1, and $.80 on each share. His total dividends for the year amounted to what percentage of the price he paid for each share?

2. Three stockholders own all the issued shares of the Harris, Lopez, and Hall Corporation. Harris has 750 shares; Lopez, 260 shares; and Hall, 490.
   a. Is this a close or an open corporation? Why?
   b. What percentage of the shares does each partner own?
   c. Which partner, if any, has control over the results of any votes that are taken? Explain.
   d. If Hall wanted total control of the corporation, how many shares would she need to buy?

3. The board of directors of Melby Company, Inc., decided to distribute $40,950 as dividends to shareholders. There are 27,300 shares of stock held by stockholders.
   a. What is the amount of the dividend to be distributed on each share?
   b. John Taylor owns 240 shares. What amount will he receive in dividends?

4. On the statement of financial position of the Fenwick Company, the assets have a value of $117,000; the debts are listed as $37,000; and the capital stock as $80,000. The company decided to go out of business. The assets are converted into $97,000 cash. What amount of cash will the stockholders receive?

5. The net profit of a retail cooperative is $4,000, and the purchases made by members amount to $100,000. If the profit is divided in proportion to the purchases, how much should be given to a member who made purchases of $1,000?

6. Alone or in teams (as specified by your instructor), search the library or the Web to gather information about the basic features of a cooperative. Then report to your class on how cooperatives differ from typical corporations as to how they operate and how the investors share in the benefits. Use a search source such as www.altavista.com or www.yahoo. In particular, go to www.rurdev.usda.gov/rbs/pub/cir55/cir55rpt.htm.

SOLVE BUSINESS PROBLEMS

CASE 6-1

Takoda Koriyama, whose parents came from Japan, is interested in how corporations operate in Western countries, particularly the United States. In one of his business classes, he and two classmates—Marcus Jordan and Brianna Ashman—were assigned a team project to study the total pay of chief executive officers (CEOs) for ten companies. Takoda is the leader. Other class teams were assigned other firms. Their assignment was to determine the total pay that individual CEOs earn in American corporations in relation to how well their firms do for their stockholders.

All three members had gathered information. Before they could prepare a class report, they need to sort it all out. During their first meeting, the group shared information and created the chart below that summarizes their main points. CEO total pay is shown in thousands of dollars.

Corporations	*CEO Total Pay*	*Percent of Shareholder Return*
Walt Disney	$ 594,892	56
Citigroup	491,976	146
General Electric	151,179	199
Occidental Petroleum	110,670	−11
H. J. Heinz	104,678	86
Immunex	2,437	663
Microsoft	1,696	532
Costco	1,483	373
Capital One	1,312	393
Berkshire Hathaway	842	118

Source: *Business Week, April 19, 1999*

Think Critically:

1. Which five company CEOs benefited their shareholders the most? And which five company CEOs benefited their shareholders the least?
2. If you had purchased shares in Occidental Petroleum, what main point would you stress in your letter as a stockholder to the chairman of the board of directors?
3. What general statement can you make to Takoda and his team about the fairness of CEO pay and their contributions to their corporations?
4. If you were just elected to serve as a board member of Citigroup, what would you recommend to other board members about the CEO's future pay? Provide a reason for your answer.
5. Which CEO would most deserve a raise in pay? Justify your answer.

6. Alone or in teams, as specified by your instructor, gather information about CEO pay from *Business Week, Fortune,* or other magazines in your library or from the Internet. Prepare a report for your class that answers the question: Are CEOs overpaid, underpaid, or paid what they are worth? Also include proposals found on how to keep CEO pay fair and under control.

CASE 6-2

Alicia Fuentes owns 15 shares of stock in the Shale Oil Company, a large corporation that deals with oil and gas products. Hugh Jones, a friend of Alicia's, owns 20 shares. Today they both received an invitation to attend the annual stockholders' meeting in Chicago, which neither can attend. This conversation occurred during the evening when they were having dinner at a local restaurant:

Alicia: *Since I can't attend the meeting, I'm going to sign the proxy card and answer "for" regarding the two proposals that are to be voted upon. Of course, I don't know any of the board members who are up for election, but they must be OK. I wish they could distribute more dividends, though.*

Hugh: *You shouldn't just give your vote away to management, Alicia. You should elect one of the candidates to be an outside board member. That person could then shake things up a bit, get some changes made. You probably also don't know anything about the other item asking for approval to increase the number of shares of stock that can be sold.*

Alicia: *I don't have time to do homework on the company. Shale Oil Company always makes a profit; therefore, it deserves my vote.*

Hugh: *Too many stockholders don't do their homework on the company, and not many go to the meetings. So, management always has its own way. Why bother sending a proxy statement at all? I'm not going to waste time sending my proxy back.*

Alicia: *I'm still going to vote, Hugh. Besides, the company pays the postage.*

Hugh: *You're doing what everyone else does. Management always wins. But since you're going to vote, I will too. The difference is that I'm going to vote against the two items . . . no, on second thought, I'll just sign the proxy. That will really confuse them.*

Think Critically:

1. Whether they vote "for" or "against" the proposals listed on the proxy statement, how many votes can Alicia and Hugh cast?

2. If the proxy statement is like the one shown in Figure 6-6 and Hugh signs it but does not mark "for" or "against" the two proposals, how do you think the management will use the proxy?
3. If Hugh or Alicia wanted an important proposal to be made known and voted upon by the stockholders, how could they achieve their goal?
4. How should Alicia and Hugh have received information about each of the proposals from management that would enable them to vote with adequate information?
5. What might an outside board member do that an inside member might not do?

PROJECT: MY BUSINESS, INC.

Corporations are another form of business ownership. In addition to financial advantages, there are other reasons to organize a new business as a corporation. In this segment of the project, you will study some of those reasons as well as the procedures necessary to form a corporation in your state.

DATA COLLECTION

1. Make a list of the legal procedures you must follow in your state to organize a close corporation to operate your business. Obtain the information from a library, the Internet, or a government office.
2. Interview the owner of a small business that has been organized as a corporation. Ask the owner to identify the advantages and disadvantages of the corporate form of ownership for a small business.
3. Identify one other form of ownership that could be appropriate for your business other than a proprietorship, partnership, or corporation. Locate a business that is organized using that ownership form and study its operations.

ANALYSIS

1. Most new small businesses are formed as proprietorships and partnerships rather than corporations. However, new corporations have a higher success rate than other types of business organizations. What might be some reasons for that higher success rate?
2. Assume that your business is successful and expands during the next five years. Identify specific situations that could occur during that five-year period in which it would be beneficial to reor-

ganize the business as a corporation. Collect and analyze the legal documents needed. Consider changing financial needs, management activities, business operations, and your own personal needs.

3. Assume you are going to organize your juice bar as a corporation. Collect and review the documents needed to register your corporation with the state and to complete the formation of the corporation.

LEGAL ASPECTS OF BUSINESS

OBJECTIVES

7-1 Explain how federal laws help control and promote competition.

7-2 Tell how patents, copyrights, and trademarks are beneficial to business.

7-3 Offer examples of how the government protects the public.

7-4 Provide three methods used by state and local governments to regulate business.

7-5 Discuss the nature of taxes and the fairness of progressive, proportional, and regressive taxes.

7-6 Identify and explain the most common types of taxes that affect business.

LEGAL LIMITS FOR A TAXI BUSINESS

eion Banks, who owned a small taxi business in his hometown, was meeting for lunch with his lawyer, Laura Maddox. He needed to discuss several matters that had occurred during the past few weeks. While waiting for the server, Laura said, "You seem quite upset."

Deion sat back and replied, "I am, Laura. Here are the new tax forms that need to be filled out. And that's the easy part. Would you check with the town officials to see why they want to review my franchise before I buy another cab? Also, while you're at the Town Hall, see what you can do to prevent those officials from giving another taxi firm a license to operate. This town isn't big enough for two taxi companies. I'll get less business, and it will probably force down my fares. If there is a chance of going bankrupt, I should probably

move my business across the river. The income tax rate in that state is much lower."

"Don't do anything drastic," said Laura. "Let me see what I can find out from our government officials. I'll get back to you in a few days with both your tax forms and the answers to your questions."

Deion Banks, like other business owners, must operate within the law. Laws that regulate business cover both products and services, and they govern general relationships of businesses with competitors, consumers, employees, and the public. Deion Banks's taxi business is no exception. He currently benefits from being the only taxi company in town, but he now feels threatened. The town may, indeed, allow someone else the right to open a competing firm. So what can Deion do?

In the following pages you will learn how government encourages free enterprise by controlling monopolies and promoting competition. You will also learn how the government protects the general public as well as business. Like Deion, you will learn about taxes and how taxes influence business decisions.

■ REGULATIONS MAINTAINING COMPETITION

Competition is the rivalry among companies for customers' dollars. Competition, however, does not always operate smoothly by itself. To provide for fair competition, government has passed laws and created regulations to enforce the laws. These laws and regulations grow out of a need to preserve competition, which is done, in part, by controlling monopolies and unfair business practices. Firms that cannot survive in a competitive atmosphere either go out of business or face bankruptcy.

■ CONTROLLING MONOPOLIES

A **monopoly** exists when only one company provides a product or service without competition from other companies. Without competitors, the one producer can control the supply and price of the product or service. By controlling the supply of an item, a single producer

QUESTION 1
Exam2

CAREER CONNECTION

LAWYER

Although the popular view of lawyers emphasizes sensational courtroom trials, many lawyers have jobs in government and in business firms, public utilities, banks, insurance companies, real estate agencies, manufacturing firms, and welfare organizations. But no matter what the situation, lawyers hold positions of great responsibility and must adhere to a strict code of ethics.

The more detailed aspects of lawyers' work have been greatly influenced by advances in technology. Software can be used to search legal literature and to organize and index material. Lawyers use the Internet, electronic filing, videoconferencing, and voice-recognition technology. These tools save time and reduce legal costs.

Formal educational requirements usually include a four-year college degree, followed by three years in law school. After that, states require that applicants pass a written bar examination. Persons interested in a particular aspect of law may find related courses useful. For example, tax lawyers must have a broad knowledge of accounting.

For more career information about lawyers, check your library or the Internet for resources.

can set a price that will generate the greatest profit. In a monopoly situation, such as Deion Banks's taxi company, the prices are generally very high. Without competitors to lure customers away with lower prices, the monopolistic company can raise its price as high as it wants. If customers want the product or service, they have no choice but to pay the monopolist's price.

In actual practice, however, few monopolies exist, because of the effectiveness of competition. To illustrate, assume a business offers a new product that no other business has. The product suddenly becomes quite popular. The prospect of profits to be made entices other companies to enter the market to help meet the demand. A temporary monopoly will exist until those competitors can produce and sell similar products. Usually, through competitive pricing, the more efficient companies will attract the greatest number of purchasers, while the less efficient may struggle for survival or go out of business. Even if some competitors fail, however, a monopoly will not exist as long as there are at least two or more producers.

In some situations, however, monopolies may be better for consumers than competition. These situations usually involve providing public services, such as public utilities, which have a fairly stable demand and which are costly to create. A natural gas company, for example, must build hundreds of miles of pipeline along streets and roads in order to deliver gas to homes and industries to fuel furnaces and stoves. If two or three gas companies incurred these same costs to sell gas to a relatively fixed number of customers, the price of gas would be higher than if only one company existed. Also, installing and maintaining so many pipelines would create nuisance problems along crowded streets and highways. In these types of situations, the government grants a monopoly to one company, regulates the prices that the company can charge, and influences other company policies.

Until recently, the federal government had approved of closely regulated monopolies, such as the postal system, utility companies, rail-

roads, and communication firms. However, the trend has shifted from allowing monopolies to weakening or eliminating them in order to encourage competition. No longer, for example, are passenger fares on commercial airlines regulated. As a result, fares have generally dropped. Even telephone service, the trucking industry, and railroads have been deregulated. Today utilities are undergoing deregulation. Firms such as MCI WorldCom and Sprint offer communication services at competitive prices and compete fiercely with the once monopolistic AT&T. The result overall has been that consumers pay lower prices and have more services from which to select.

PROMOTING FAIR COMPETITION   One way to promote competition is to limit the number of monopolies created and controlled by government. Monopoly conditions can also arise when businesses compete too harshly or unfairly. A large, powerful business can lower its prices deliberately to drive out competitors, thereby discouraging competition. Thus, the federal government supports business practices that encourage competition and discourage monopolies. To achieve this goal, government has passed important laws and created agencies to enforce the laws.

Sherman Act. The first major law promoting competition was the Sherman Antitrust Act of 1890. One of its primary purposes is to discourage monopolies by outlawing business agreements among competitors that might tend to promote monopolies. For example, agreements among competitors to set selling prices on goods are unlawful. If three sellers met and agreed to set the same selling price on the same product each sold, they would all be violating the Sherman Act.

QUESTION 3 Exam 2

Clayton Act. Like the Sherman Act, the Clayton Act of 1914 was aimed at discouraging monopolies. One part of the law forbids corporations from acquiring ownership rights in other corporations if the purpose is to create a monopoly or to discourage competition. Corporation A cannot, for example, buy over half the ownership rights of its main competitor, Corporation B, if the aim is to severely reduce or eliminate competition.

Another section of the Clayton Act forbids business contracts that require customers to purchase certain goods in order to get other goods. For example, a business that produces computers cannot require a buyer also to purchase supplies, such as paper and software, in order to get a computer. Microsoft Corporation was charged with such a violation. Microsoft required computer makers that wanted to buy its dominant Windows operating system to also accept its Internet Explorer browser. The result of this action was to severely damage the sales of Netscape's Navigator browser, which was Microsoft's dominant competitor.

Robinson-Patman Act. The Robinson-Patman Act of 1936 amended the portion of the Clayton Act dealing with the pricing of goods. The main purpose of the pricing provisions in both of these laws is to prevent **price discrimination**—setting different prices for different customers. For example, a seller cannot offer a price of $5 a unit to Buyer A and sell the same goods to Buyer B at $6 a unit. Different prices can be set, however, if the goods sold are different in quality or quantity. Buyer A is entitled to the $5 price if the quantity purchased is significantly greater or if the quality is lower. The same discounts must then be offered to all buyers purchasing the same quantity or quality as Buyer A.

Wheeler-Lea Act. In 1938, the Wheeler-Lea Act was passed to strengthen earlier laws outlawing unfair methods of competition. This law made unfair or deceptive acts or practices, including false advertising, unlawful. **False advertising** is advertising that is misleading in some important way, including the failure to reveal facts about possible results from using the advertised products. Under the Wheeler-Lea Act, it is unlawful for an advertiser to circulate false advertising that can lead to the purchase of foods, drugs, medical devices, or cosmetics, or to participate in any other unfair methods of competition.

QUESTION 2 Exam2

FEDERAL TRADE COMMISSION The Federal Trade Commission (FTC) was created as the result of many businesses demanding protection from unfair methods of competition. The FTC administers most of the federal laws dealing with fair competition. Some of the unfair practices that the FTC protects businesses from are shown in Figure 7-1.

QUESTION 5 EXAM2

OTHER FEDERAL AGENCIES In addition to the FTC, the federal government has created other agencies to administer laws that regulate specialized areas of business, such as transportation and communication. Figure 7-2 lists some of the more important agencies.

■ PROVIDING BANKRUPTCY RELIEF

All firms face the risk of failure. The free enterprise system permits unsuccessful businesses to file for bankruptcy as a means of protect-

1. Any act that restrains trade.
2. Any monopolies except those specifically authorized by law, such as public utilities.
3. Price fixing, such as agreements among competitors.
4. Agreements among competitors to divide territory, earnings, or profits.
5. Gaining control over the supply of any commodity in order to create an artificial scarcity.
6. False or misleading advertising.
7. Imitation of trademark or trade name.
8. Discrimination through prices or special deals.
9. Pretending to sell at a discount when there is no reduction in price.
10. Offering so-called free merchandise with a purchase when the price of the article sold has been raised to compensate for the free merchandise.
11. Misrepresentation about the quality, the composition, or the place of origin of a product.
12. Violation of one's guarantee of privacy of information on the Internet, including e-mail.

FIGURE 7-1

Types of Practices Prohibited by the Federal Trade Commission

Some Federal Agencies That Regulate Business

AGENCY AND REGULATION

FIGURE 7-2

Laws promoting fair practices that benefit businesses and consumers are enforced by government agencies.

Federal Aviation Administration

Safety standards, airplane accidents, and take-offs and landings

Federal Communications Commission

Radio, television, telephone, telegraph, cable, and satellite communications

Food and Drug Administration

Foods, drugs, medical devices, cosmetics, and veterinary products

Nuclear Regulatory Commission

Nuclear power plants

Securities and Exchange Commission

Stocks and bonds

QUESTION 7
Exam2

Various federal agencies have been created to administer laws that regulate specialized areas of business. Which federal agency regulates communications?

In 1998, 44,367 U.S. businesses filed for bankruptcy. The state with the most business bankruptcy filings was California; the state with the least filings was North Dakota.

ing owners and others. **Bankruptcy** is a legal process that allows the selling of assets to pay off debts. Businesses as well as individuals can file for bankruptcy. If cash is not available to pay the debts after assets are sold, the law excuses the business or individual from paying the remaining unpaid debts. In such a case, all those to whom money was owed would very likely receive less than the full amount.

A bankruptcy judge can permit a company to survive bankruptcy proceedings if a survival plan can be developed that might enable the firm to recover. As a result, after starting bankruptcy proceedings, many firms do survive. However, bankruptcy carries serious consequences. The business will have a bad credit rating. A record of the unpaid debts will stay on file for ten years, and the business may not file for bankruptcy again for six years. As a result, the business will have difficulty obtaining credit.

■ REGULATIONS PROTECTING BUSINESS AND THE PUBLIC

In the previous section, you learned about regulations that help to make the economic system work by establishing rules of fair competition. In this section, you will learn about regulations that protect those who create goods and services and those who use them.

■ PROTECTING BUSINESS

The federal government has passed laws to protect the rights of those who create uniquely different products and new ideas. Specifically, it grants intellectual property rights to inventors, authors, and creators of distinct symbols and names for goods and services (see Figure 7-3).

PATENTS A **patent** is an agreement in which the federal government gives an inventor the sole right for 20 years to make, use, and sell an invention or a process. No one is permitted to copy or use the invention without permission. This protection is a reward for the time and money invested to create the new product. An inventor may allow others to make or use a product by giving them a license to do so.

QUESTION 9
Exam2

In a sense, through the Patent and Trademark Office, the government gives the inventor a monopoly on newly invented products, designs, and processes. This temporary monopoly provides a profit incentive that encourages manufacturers to spend the huge amounts of money required to research and develop new ideas. Research departments have produced many inventions. For example, Sony and other camera companies have developed digital cameras that allow users to see their pictures on a special display screen and even edit them before they ever leave the camera. Even synthetic tissue and altered vegetable plants are patentable. For example, insulin that diabetics need and a new rot-resistant tomato are products of biotechnology (biology plus technology) innovations.

New processes as well as new products can be patented, but process patenting can be undesirable at times. For example, Priceline.com, Inc., received a patent for its auction price bidding system on the Internet. If other companies used this simple process, they would be violating the owner's patent rights. However, the process is so fundamental to many Internet practices that competitors believe the patent is essentially unfair. Should doctors who develop a new method for healing people

Intellectual Property

PATENTS

Motors
Mousetraps
Games
Computers

COPYRIGHTS

Software
Novels
Histories
Poetry
Textbooks

TRADEMARKS

Names
Symbols

FIGURE 7-3

Federal, state, and local governments grant special property rights.

prohibit other doctors from using it or require them to pay a licensing fee? Occasionally the Patent and Trademark Office revokes or denies patents that discourage desirable competition.

Unfortunately, stealing patents is an acceptable practice in some countries that do not honor the U.S. patent law. As a result, American firms lose millions of dollars. By tightening trade agreements with these countries, this great loss to American firms may begin to decline. On the other hand, patent laws differ worldwide. For example, Japan's patents promote technology sharing, whereas U.S. patents protect inventors.

COPYRIGHTS   A **copyright** is similar to a patent in that the federal government gives an author the sole right to reproduce, publish, and sell literary or artistic work for the life of the author, typically, plus 70 years. No one may publish or reproduce copyrighted work without permission of the copyright owner. However, the law permits occasional photocopying of copyrighted material. While a teacher could copy a magazine article to distribute to students, articles from the same magazine could not be copied and distributed weekly throughout the school year without obtaining permission.

Copyright laws also cover electronic methods for distributing creative work. Copyrights protect creators of CD games and music, video and audio tapes, and computer software programs, for example. Duplicating CDs, tapes, disks, and software programs for distribution to others is usually illegal. When an employee makes a personal copy of a computer software program for use on a home computer, the employee violates the copyright law. Furthermore, if a warning is not publicized that copying creative work such as a software program is illegal, the employer is also guilty.

Copyrights are regulated by the federal

> QUESTION 11
> Exam 2

> QUESTION 4
> Exam 2

ILLUSTRATION 7-3

What kinds of laws protect the duplication and distribution of computer software?

Copyright Office. Like a patent, a copyright is a special type of monopoly granted to authors, publishers, and other creators of original works. An example of a copyright notice appears on the back of the title page in the front of this book.

TRADEMARKS Trademarks are like patents because they are special types of monopolies. A **trademark** is a distinguishing name, symbol, or special mark placed on a good or service that is legally reserved for the sole use of the owner. Many nationally known products have trademarks that most people recognize. Some trademarks are symbols, such as the Nike "swoosh" or the McDonald's "golden arches." Others are company or product names, such as the Sony "Walkman" or Nintendo's "Game Boy." Trademarks, like patents, are regulated by the Patent and Trademark Office.

■ PROTECTING THE PUBLIC

The federal government protects the legal rights of not only those who create new products and ideas but also those who consume goods and services. Two major goals of legislation are to ensure safe products for consumers and prevent the misuse of information.

FOOD AND DRUGS Products related to the human body are closely regulated. The Food and Drug Administration administers the Federal Food, Drug, and Cosmetic Act and related laws. These laws prohibit the sale of impure, improperly labeled, falsely guaranteed, and unhealthful foods, drugs, and cosmetics. Producers of cosmetics, for example, must show that their products will not harm users. Should a product cause harm, the Food and Drug Administration may require the producer to stop its sale or to notify the public of its possible danger.

NON-FOOD PRODUCTS Legislative activity dealing with the safety of non-food products has increased in recent years. Laws now require labels on many products if possible danger exists from product use. A health warning message, for example, must appear on cigarette packages. The FTC forbids the sale of tobacco and smokeless tobacco to those under 18 because research shows that the majority of those who smoke when young die prematurely of smoking-related diseases. Also, auto and highway safety laws exist to reduce death and injury.

The Consumer Product Safety Act sets safety standards on many items. When products already sold are found to have a dangerous defect, businesses are legally required to recall, repair, or stop selling the products. Dangerous toys, for example, have been removed from the market. And recalls have occurred with such products as cars and sports utility vehicles. A federal Warranty Act requires sellers to specify what they will or will not do if their product is defective. Many product liability laws also exist at the state level.

QUESTION 13 Exam2

FACTS AND FIGURES

Trademark rights may continue indefinitely, as long as the mark is neither abandoned by the trademark owner nor loses its significance in the marketplace as a trademark by becoming a generic term. For example, the generic terms "escalator," "linoleum," and "zipper" were once trademarks.

ETHICAL ISSUES

ETHICS AND INTERNET ADVERTISING

The Internet is a popular place to browse for general information and to buy products or services. But as the Internet grows in popularity, buyers have become concerned about the privacy of their personal information and its possible misuse. Are buyers' fears justified?

DoubleClick, or DC, is a provider of advertising services to retailers who sell their wares to Internet shoppers. DC has over 2,300 business customers including Ford, Levi-Strauss, and NBC.

DC's clients want to target their Internet advertising to the people most likely to buy their products. DC can identify, for example, which potential customers might buy Ford cars online. The main way to identify these buyers is through "cookies"—files stored on customers' computers. The cookies collect information on what customers buy and where they go on the Web, revealing their preferences and buying habits.

DC manages the advertising for its client businesses, and from the customer information it connects online, it selects the customers that best match a firm's target audience. DC uses the customer information it collects to help its clients advertise effectively.

DC requires its business customers to collect information from customers when they make sales. DC itself claims not to collect personally identifiable information about people, such as names, addresses, and telephone numbers. It does collect non-personally identifiable information, such as whether people have responded to an advertisement and the type of computer system that they use. The non-personal information is used to measure advertisement effectiveness for DC's business clients. Internet customers have a choice of whether to forbid, restrict, or deny the use of information stored in cookies. Clear notice must be given customers, so that they can make their decisions.

DoubleClick is planning to merge with Abacus Direct, a company that has a massive collection of the catalog-buying habits of more than 80 million families, including names, addresses, and telephone numbers. This information can permit DC's business clients to target these people with e-mail advertising. Some consumer groups have objected strongly, claiming that this is an invasion of privacy that should be stopped. The Federal Trade Commission has initiated an investigation.

THINK CRITICALLY

1. Identify three people who have purchased an item on the Internet. Ask these people if they had read the privacy policy before purchasing and if they know what a "cookie" is. Report your findings to the class.
2. Do the selling methods of Internet advertisers invade your privacy any more than do companies who mail you advertising or call you at home to try to sell you their products? Defend your answer.
3. A very young person is often not concerned about what information he or she provides to others on the Internet. How could an unethical business capture and use this information in a way that could harm the family?

INFORMATION Businesses need information. This need has resulted in the heavy use of computers to manage data. Vast amounts of information from many sources are collected, processed, stored, and distributed by computer, especially on the Internet. As a result, individuals and businesses need protection from the wrongful use of private information.

Stores check credit card balances, banks check credit ratings, hospitals store patients' health records electronically, and the government collects income tax data on all taxpayers. Incorrect information in any of these sensitive records could be very damaging to the individual. Also, only authorized people should have access to such highly personal information.

Therefore, businesses that extensively use computer information must handle information carefully to protect the rights of individuals and organizations. Carelessly handled information can lead to **information liability**—the responsibility for physical or economic injury arising from incorrect data or wrongful use of data.

QUESTION 15
Exam 2

Information liability is similar to product liability. If a defective product injures someone, the injured party can sue the producer of the product. Similarly, if a person's credit rating suffers because an employee keys a social security number into a credit record incorrectly, the business is liable for creating the problem. Also, a company not directly involved in collecting or recording incorrect information may, however, be held liable for distributing it. For instance, if a store gives an incorrect credit balance to a bank that results in the refusal for a loan, the bank is as liable as the store that provided the incorrect information.

Occasionally, someone tampers with computerized data. The Electronic Communications Privacy Act and related laws make it a crime for any unauthorized person to access a major computer system and view, use, or change data. The laws deal with the interception and disclosure of electronic communications, including e-mail privacy. Privacy laws help protect the public from the wrongful use or misuse of information.

A debate continues over the electronic collection of information over the Internet. Web sites can place small files called "cookies" on the computers of site visitors without their knowledge. **Cookies** are files of information about the user that some Web sites create and store on the user's own computer. These cookies can, among other things, track where users go on the Net to gather information on interests and preferences for marketing purposes. Some people feel that such data gathering is an invasion of privacy. The companies argue that they are simply identifying what consumers want so they can better serve them.

■ STATE AND LOCAL REGULATIONS

The federal government regulates interstate commerce while the individual states regulate intrastate commerce. **Interstate commerce** is defined as business operations and transactions that cross state lines,

ILLUSTRATION 7-4

How could the concept of information liability affect the way in which a business handles computer information?

QUESTION 17
Exam 2

such as products that are produced in one state and sold in other states. **Intrastate commerce,** on the other hand, is defined as business transacted within a state. Most small service firms are involved mainly in intrastate commerce, since they usually sell to customers located within the same state. Because most large companies are likely to be involved in both interstate and intrastate commerce, they are subject to state and federal regulations.

Moreover, each state has a constitution that allows it to create other governing units, such as cities, towns, and counties. These units also regulate business transacted within them. Large businesses especially are subject to local, state, and federal laws.

Many state and local laws are related to federal laws. Most states, for instance, have laws that promote competition, protect consumers and the environment, safeguard the public's health, and improve employment conditions. In addition, however, state and local governments regulate business by issuing licenses, franchises, and building codes, and by passing zoning regulations.

■ LICENSING

State and local governments have used **licensing** as a way to limit and control those who plan to enter certain types of businesses. To start a business that requires a license, the owner must file an application. If the government believes there is a sufficient number of these kinds of businesses, the application can be refused.

Business is regulated not only by the granting of licenses but also by regular inspections by government officials to see that the company is operated according to the law. If it is not being properly operated, it can lose its license. For example, government agents inspect a licensed restaurant from time to time for cleanliness. If the restaurant fails inspection, the government may withdraw its license, and the restaurant would have to close.

Licensing laws vary from place to place. In some cities, businesses of all types must obtain licenses, while in other communities only certain types need licenses. It is particularly common to license restaurants, beauty salons, health and fitness centers, barber shops, and other types of service firms that may affect the health of customers. In most states and in many cities, licensing laws regulate the sale of such items as liquor and tobacco.

Businesses may also license the use of property. For example, a computer software company may give a business a license to use and copy a software program in return for a fee. Likewise, for a fee a business may license another firm to make a product using its patented device. Even firm names can be licensed. For example, Walt Disney Productions licenses its animal characters for use on clothing and other products.

■ PUBLIC FRANCHISING

Another way for state and local governments to control business is through public franchises. A **public franchise** is a contract that permits a person or organization to use public property for private profit. No individual member of society, however, has a right to use public property for profit except through a special grant by society. Cities often grant public franchises to companies to operate bus lines, or to install electric power or cable for television. For example, as presented in the story that started this chapter, Deion has a franchise from his community to operate his taxi company.

■ BUILDING CODES AND ZONING

Local governments regulate business through **building codes,** which control physical features of structures. Building codes may specify such things as the maximum height, minimum square feet of space, and the types of materials that can be used. Local governments also regulate the types of buildings and where they are built. **Zoning** regulations specify which land areas may be used for homes and which areas may be used for different types of businesses. A business must obey all local regulations relating to zoning and construction.

■ BUSINESS TAXES

While government uses many different ways to regulate business, no way is more important than taxes. The types and amounts of taxes

During the 1990s, Disney's licensing business became a victim of its own success. The strategy during the first half of the 1990s was geared around such animated hit films as "Beauty and the Beast," "Aladdin," and "The Lion King." Licensees reached a peak of more than 4,000. This became far too many relationships to manage. Disney eventually cut the number of licensees in half. By having broader relationships with fewer licensees, Disney was able to more effectively build new merchandise campaigns to strengthen established characters like Mickey Mouse and Winnie the Pooh.

Question 6
Exam 2

Question 19
Exam 2

influence business decisions that, in turn, can influence the total amount of business activity for a region and for the nation.

Both businesses and individuals pay many kinds of taxes to local, state, and federal governments. Taxes collected by the federal government account for about 56 percent of all taxes collected, while various state and local taxes account for the remaining 44 percent. Most corporations pay nearly one half of their profits in various kinds of taxes.

■ GENERAL NATURE OF TAXES

Government levies taxes for different reasons. When government decides to levy a particular type of tax, it must consider fairness to taxpayers.

REASONS FOR TAXES Governments use taxes mainly to raise revenue (money) to fund new and ongoing programs. Governments also use taxes to regulate business activity.

Governments set revenue goals that must be reached in order to provide the various services desired by the public. Examples of these services range from law enforcement and road building to providing for the military defense of the country. It is costly for government to provide the many services the public wants. To pay for these services, therefore, it must collect taxes.

ILLUSTRATION 7-5

For what purposes do governments use taxes?

Governments also use taxes to control business activity. They can speed up economic growth by lowering taxes and slow it by raising taxes. The federal government also taxes certain foreign goods that enter this country in order to encourage consumers to purchase American-made rather than foreign-made products. State and local governments also control business activity through taxation. For example, they often set high taxes on alcoholic beverages and tobacco, in part, to discourage customers from purchasing these products.

FAIRNESS OF TAXATION   It is difficult for government to find ways to levy taxes fairly and still raise sufficient amounts of money to meet government expenses. The question of fairness has caused many debates. One problem is determining who will, in fact, pay the tax. For example, a firm may have to pay taxes on the goods it manufactures. But, since the tax is part of the cost of producing the product, this cost may be passed on to the customer. Another problem of fairness is whether those with the most assets or most income should pay at a higher rate than those who own or earn the least. Government tries to solve the fairness problem by adopting a proportional, progressive, or regressive tax policy.

Proportional Taxation. A **proportional tax**—sometimes called a **flat tax**—is one in which the tax rate remains the same regardless of the amount on which the tax is imposed. For example, in a given area the tax rate on real estate per $1,000 of property value is always the same, regardless of the amount of real estate the taxpayer owns. The total dollar amount of the tax paid by someone with a $400,000 home will differ from that paid by the person with a $175,000 home in the same area, but the rate of the tax is the same for both owners. A flat state tax of 6 percent on income is also proportional. Those with higher incomes pay more dollars than those with lower incomes. But the tax rate of 6 percent stays the same.

Progressive Taxation. A **progressive tax** is a tax based on the ability to pay. The policy of progressive taxation is a part of many state and federal income tax systems. As income increases, the tax rate increases. As a result, a lower-income person is taxed at a lower rate than a higher-income person is. In fact, the Tax Foundation found that in a recent year, 5 percent of the taxpayers that pay the most taxes contributed over half of all the federal individual income taxes collected.

Question 20 Exam 2

Some local and state governments have combined the policies of proportional and progressive taxes. For example, a state may apply a flat tax of 5 percent to incomes up to $20,000 and 6 percent to all incomes over $20,000.

The current federal tax law is a combination of progressive and proportional taxation policy. A 15 percent tax applies to taxable income up to $43,050 for married couples filing joint returns. On taxable income from $43,050 and up to $104,050, the rate jumps to 28 percent. With still higher incomes, the rate jumps within brackets to 31 percent, 36 percent, and 39.6 percent, respectively. For single taxpayers, the rate is 15 percent up to $25,750. On taxable income from $25,750 to $62,450, the tax rate is 28 percent. Tax rates continue to rise within brackets to 31 percent, 36 percent, and then 39.6 percent, respectively, for people with higher taxable incomes. Because people with higher incomes pay more than those with lower incomes, most people consider the tax fair.

Regressive Taxation. The third type of tax policy is a **regressive tax.** With this type of tax, the actual tax rate decreases as the taxable amount increases. While general sales taxes are often thought to be proportional, they are actually regressive, because people with lower incomes pay a larger proportion of their incomes in taxes than those with higher incomes. Suppose, for example, that A and B live in a state with a 6 percent general sales tax. As shown in Figure 7-4, Person A with an annual take-home pay of $15,000 pays a 6 percent tax rate, while Person B with an annual take-home pay of $45,000 pays only a 5.7 percent tax rate. Because the sales tax applies to purchases rather than to income, the general sales tax is regressive. For a less regressive sales tax, some states exclude taxes on such purchases as food and clothing. These exclusions are usually items on which low-income families spend a high percentage of their income.

FIGURE 7-4

People with very high incomes often prefer regressive taxes.

	PERSON A	PERSON B
Take-Home Pay	$15,000	$45,000
State Sales Tax	6%	6%
Take-Home Pay Not Spent	0	$2,000
Take-Home Pay Spent	$15,000	$43,000
Tax Calculation	($15,000 x .06)	($43,000 x .06)
Tax	$900	$2,580
Tax Rate Calculation	($900 ÷ $15,000)	($2,580 ÷ $45,000)
Effective Tax Rate	6%	5.7%

KINDS OF TAXES

Taxation has become so complicated that the average businessperson spends a great deal of time filling out tax forms, computing taxes, and filing various reports. In many businesses, various taxes reduce a great percentage of their income. The three most common types of taxes affecting businesses and individuals are income taxes, sales taxes, and property taxes. Figure 7-5 gives examples of the types of taxes that a business operating in only one state may be required to pay.

INCOME TAX   The federal government and most state governments use the income tax to raise revenues. An **income tax** is a tax on the profits of businesses and on earnings of individuals. For individuals, the tax is based on salaries and other income earned after certain deductions. For businesses, an income tax usually applies to net profits (receipts less expenses).

The income tax is the largest source of revenue for the federal government. While individuals pay about 70 percent of the total federal income taxes collected, businesses pay nearly all of the remaining 30 percent. Businesses share the cost of collecting individual income taxes. Every business is required to withhold income taxes from employees' earnings and turn it over to the government. Thus, business performs an important tax service for government. Individuals and businesses pay lower rates in the U.S. than in most other developed nations, as shown in Figure 7-6.

QUESTION 18 Exam 2

SALES TAX   A **sales tax** is a tax levied on the retail price of goods and services at the time they are sold. A general sales tax usually applies to all goods or services sold by retailers. However, when a sales tax applies only to selected goods or services, such as cigarettes and gasoline, it is called an **excise tax.**

Sales taxes are the main source of revenue for most states and some cities and counties. Although state governments do not all administer sales taxes in the same way, in most cases the retail business collects

QUESTION 8 Exam 2

Assessments	Payroll taxes
Corporation taxes	Property tax—intangible property
Federal excise tax	Property tax— merchandise
Federal social security tax	Property tax— personal
Federal income tax	Property tax— real estate
Franchise tax	Sales tax
Gasoline tax	Severance tax
Licenses	State income tax
Local income tax	State unemployment tax
Motor truck licenses and taxes	State workers' insurance tax

FIGURE 7-5

The Most Common Business Taxes

Major Taxes for Selected Countries (in Percent)

Sweden	55.6%
France	47.6
Belgium	46.1
Germany	44.1
Canada	37.2
Britain	35.5
Greece	33.9
United States	31.7
Japan	29.0

Source: *Statistical Abstract of the United States, 1998*

FIGURE 7-6

U.S. tax rates are relatively low in comparison to those of other nations.

QUESTION 16
Exam 2

the tax from customers and turns this tax over to the state government. A business must be familiar with the sales tax law of the state in which it operates so that it can collect and report the tax properly.

From time to time, federal officials have considered charging a national sales tax. State officials, however, strongly oppose a national sales tax because that is their primary source of tax revenues. The question as to how and whether to tax Internet sales is also under debate between the states and the federal government. Both see this source of taxes as highly attractive. Traditional retailers, however, who pay sales taxes believe it is unfair for Internet sales not to be taxed.

PROPERTY TAX A **property tax** is a tax on material goods owned. While the sales tax is the primary source of revenue for most state governments, the property tax is the main source of revenue for most local governments. There may be a real property tax and a personal property tax. A **real property tax** is a tax on real estate, which is land and buildings. A **personal property tax** is a tax on possessions that are moveable, such as furniture, machinery, and equipment. Essentially, personal property is anything that is not real estate. In some states there is a special property tax on raw materials used to make goods and on finished goods available for sale.

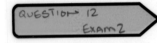

QUESTION 12
Exam 2

A tax on property—whether it is real property or personal property—is stated in terms of dollars per hundred of assessed valuation.

Assessed valuation is the value of property determined by tax officials. Thus, a tax rate of $2.80 per $100 on property with an assessed valuation of $180,000 is $5,040 ($180,000/100 = $1,800; $1,800 X $2.80 = $5,040).

QUESTION 10 Exam 2

QUESTION 14 Exam 2

■ EFFECT OF TAXES ON BUSINESS DECISIONS

Businesses consider taxes in many of their major decisions. Taxes may influence the accounting method a business selects to calculate profits and the method used to pay managers. Often, taxes are used as a basis for deciding where to locate a new business or whether to move a business from one location to another.

For example, assume that a producer of garden tools is trying to decide in which of two cities to locate a new factory. City A is located in a state that has a low state income tax and low property taxes. City B is located in a state that has no state income tax but has high property taxes. After weighing all the factors, the producer has decided to locate in City A. City A, which has both an income tax and a property tax, has been selected mainly because the total tax cost each year is less than in City B.

CHAPTER CONCEPTS

■ The federal, state, and local governments regulate business activities to protect citizens and businesses. At the national level, the Federal Trade Commission administers federal laws that regulate commerce. Landmark laws such as the Sherman and Clayton Acts helped set the stage for defining fair competition. Other federal agencies regulate basic industries such as aviation, communications, and food and drugs.

■ A primary activity of the Federal Trade Commission is to govern both publicly controlled monopolies such as utility companies and natural business monopolies. But the U.S. and other countries are moving more toward deregulation to reduce the number of public monopolies. Although the government promotes competition, there is a price to pay for business failures. A downside of free enterprise is that some firms go bankrupt, but bankruptcy laws allow businesses to recover or to exit business operations fairly. Also, when firms destroy major competitors to eliminate competition, they become monopolies and may be penalized in some way.

■ The federal government protects individuals and firms from the theft or misuse of their inventions, publications, and other intellectual property by granting the owners patents, trademarks, or copyrights. Local and state governments also regulate business through licenses, zoning laws, and franchising regulations.

■ Governments obtain revenues through taxes to pay for public services, such as police, schools, and other human services. The most common sources of revenue are income, sales, and property taxes.

■ The fairness of taxes is based mostly on what is being taxed and who pays, but the meaning of fairness is subject to debate. A progressive tax such as an income tax is based on one's ability to pay, and levies a higher tax on those who earn more and than on those who earn less. A proportional tax such as a county's real estate tax is one in which the tax rate stays the same regardless of a property's current value. A regressive tax, such as a sales tax, is a tax that requires people who earn less to pay a greater portion of their income than do people who earn more. Arguments can be made for each of the three types of taxes.

BUILD VOCABULARY POWER

Define the following terms and concepts.

1. monopoly
2. price discrimination
3. false advertising
4. bankruptcy
5. patent
6. copyright
7. trademark
8. information liability
9. cookies
10. interstate commerce

11. intrastate commerce
12. licensing
13. public franchise
14. building codes
15. zoning
16. proportional tax (flat tax)
17. progressive tax
18. regressive tax
19. income tax
20. sales tax
21. excise tax
22. property tax
23. real property tax
24. personal property tax
25. assessed valuation

REVIEW FACTS

1. When does a monopoly exist?
2. What is the name of the first major law promoting competition and in what year was it passed?
3. Which federal law forbids corporations from acquiring ownership rights in other corporations if the purpose is to create a monopoly or to discourage competition?
4. What is the main purpose of the Robinson-Patman Act of 1936?
5. Which act makes it unlawful for an advertiser to circulate false advertising that can lead to the purchase of foods, drugs, medical devices, or cosmetics, or to participate in any other unfair methods of competition?
6. How is it possible for a business to continue operating even though it has filed for bankruptcy?
7. Name five federal agencies that regulate business activities.
8. What type of agreement gives an inventor the sole right for 20 years to make, use, and sell an invention?
9. How are patents and trademarks alike?
10. Name the federal agency that protects the consumer from dangerous food and non-food products.
11. How is product liability like information liability?
12. Give two reasons why governments impose taxes.
13. Would the federal income tax be considered a regressive tax? Why or why not?
14. In which tax policy does the actual rate of taxation decrease as the taxable amount increases?
15. What are the three most common types of business taxes?

DISCUSS IDEAS

1. Discuss how a business that has a monopoly on a good or service can keep its prices unreasonably high.
2. Why is it necessary for the federal government to pass laws promoting fair competition?
3. Determine whether the following situation violates one of the antitrust laws and, if it does, identify the law that it violates. Pinter, Inc., makes one type of flashlight and sells it mostly to large retail stores. For Stores A, B, and C it sells in about the same

quantity at the same price. It also sells to Store D in about the same quantity but at a much lower price because it has been doing business with Store D longer.

4. Name at least three different practices that are prohibited under the laws administered by the Federal Trade Commission.

5. Explain how a computer software program might be both copyrighted and licensed.

6. What must a business do to protect itself from possible lawsuits if many of its employees have personal computers at home?

7. Sundial Products placed an advertisement in the local newspaper stating that its latest suntan lotion would give a deep suntan within 24 hours, without any danger to the user's health. Within a week, ten people were badly burned by the product.
   a. In what unfair practice did Sundial engage?
   b. Discuss how the federal government might control this company and its new product.

8. Monica Lopez wants to start a sewing business in her home where she can alter clothes and sell sewing supplies. Discuss whether the local zoning law that forbids her from using her home as a business is fair or unfair.

9. Which do you think is the fairest kind of tax—a proportional tax, a progressive tax, or a regressive tax? Support your answer.

10. Discuss how a local community can attract or discourage new businesses through property taxes and/or controls.

11. Amazon.com received a patent in 1999 for its "one click" shopping cart technology that simplifies buying a series of items on the Internet. Barnes and Noble bookstore and other companies have copied this technology without approval from Amazon.com. Using newspapers, magazines, or the Internet, investigate this problem and report on what may be happening or has happened with any lawsuits that may have been filed against the "copy cats."

ANALYZE INFORMATION

1. Three manufacturers that sell nationally discuss prices of a product that they all manufacture but which has become unprofitable to each. They believe that it is foolish to sell at a loss. They all agree to raise prices, but they do not agree on how much each will charge. Do you consider this action illegal? Explain.

2. Two of your friends were working in the school's computer lab one day. Because they received a failing grade on a major test, they figured out how to break into the school's computer containing student grades. Your friends were about to raise their grades and then asked you which grades you wanted changed.
   a. Discuss the ethics of changing grades.
   b. Discuss the legality of changing grades.

c. If someone got into the system and lowered a student's grades, causing the student to be rejected by a specific college, how might a judge decide if the student sued the school?

d. Can the school sue the students who changed the records? And what law might be used?

3. You live in a state that has the following tax schedule:

Taxable Income	Rate
$0-$6,999	no tax
7,000-14,999	5%
15,000-24,999	6%
25,000 and over	7%

Your state permits everyone to have $2,000 of exemptions from total income to arrive at taxable income. Your taxable income this year is only $12,000 because of work lost due to illness. Your friend's income is $19,000.

a. What is your tax this year? What is your friend's tax?

b. What is the actual tax rate you and your friend paid this year based on your total incomes?

4. If the real estate tax rate is $3.40 per $100 of assessed valuation:

a. What is the tax per $1,000 of valuation?

b. What is the tax on real estate valued at $150,000?

c. Using your local tax rate, compute the real estate tax on real estate valued at $150,000.

5. A married couple filed a joint return and had a taxable income of $45,000 after taking allowable deductions.

a. Under the federal income tax law described in this chapter, calculate their tax.

b. Calculate their tax rate if their total annual income before deductions had been $50,000.

6. Use the library or the Internet to research the history of the Sherman Antitrust Act. What unethical business practices led to the passage of this law?

7. At the library or online, look up the Consumer Bill of Rights first proposed by President John F. Kennedy. What rights are covered? What responsibilities accompany these rights?

SOLVE BUSINESS PROBLEMS

CASE 7-1

Hitesh Nazami owns and operates a hardware store in a community of 50,000 people. The nearest town is at least 25 miles away, but there are two competitors in the area, one of which is a large Home Depot. All usually run weekly advertisements.

Today, a customer he had never seen before came into the store. "I certainly hope you carry Weaver tools," the customer said. "The other stores in town don't carry the Weaver brand."

"Sure, we carry Weaver," answered Hitesh. "It's one of my best lines."

The customer looked happy and relieved, and went to his truck to get the old tool he wanted to replace. While the customer was outside, Hitesh had a chance to think about what the customer had said. Now Hitesh knew why the Weaver brand was so popular in his store. As a result, he decided to raise prices on Weaver tools by tomorrow morning. Also, he could promote Weaver tools in next week's advertisements. A smile crossed Hitesh's face as the customer returned.

"Here's the tool," said the customer. "I hope you can replace it. As you can see, it's quite different from the other brands."

"I can see that it's different," Hitesh responded. "You're lucky to get it at this low price. The price will be going up in the very near future."

Think Critically:
1. Does Hitesh have a monopoly on Weaver tools in his community?
2. If Hitesh raises his price by very much, what might happen?
3. Is raising the price suddenly (and for the reason given) an unfair business practice? Discuss.

CASE 7-2

Barbara Turner worked at the Dyme Corporation, where she negotiated sales terms and coordinated all large contracts. Jeff Collins had also worked for Dyme, but last Monday he just started working at a new company, Destiny, Inc. Barbara and Jeff had been good friends for some time.

His new company hired Jeff because he was an excellent computer person and they believed he would be valuable to the firm. During the second week, Jeff's boss informed him that the company was competing against a major rival for a rather large contract. Jeff was not told the name of the competing firm. His boss wondered whether Jeff could find out more about such contract proposals from his former employer. "The sooner the better," he said. "Any information would be extremely helpful."

That evening Jeff decided to e-mail Barbara from his home computer and ask a few questions. After an exchange of a few messages, Barbara said that recently she had been helping others develop new proposals. "In fact, we're working on a new one now and it's for a large amount." She was sure that Jeff's small company would not be making an offer of this size. "I'll receive the final details from our people by e-mail tomorrow, check them over, and then mail it to our client tomorrow morning. I can share that with you, Jeff, but I can't provide price information. In a few days I'll send the document along."

Jeff replied, "Thanks, Barbara," and closed down his computer.

The next morning Jeff's impatient boss asked him what he had learned. Jeff answered, "Give me a little more time, and I'll try to forward the information to you." A little later he tapped into Barbara's e-mail messages, found the actual proposal—with prices—and without examining it, forwarded it immediately to his boss. The boss's impatience and Jeff's desire to serve the firm well caused him to disregard Barbara's statement about prices. Later, his boss thanked Jeff immensely and commented that the firm would not forget him when bonus time came. Later the next day Barbara sent Jeff the proposal without prices. A week later Jeff's boss gleefully announced that "we got that big contract with the Crown Hill Company." Somewhat shocked by the news, Jeff now worried about what had occurred, because the proposal he got from Barbara was also for Crown Hill. "What have I done?" he asked himself.

Think Critically:

1. Assume the CEO of Dyme Corporation found out about what happened and he decided to sue Destiny, Inc. If you were Dyme's lawyer, what law would you use?

2. Who was the most unethical person, Jeff or Jeff's boss? Explain.

3. Assume Jeff calls Barbara and asks to have lunch with her to explain what happened and to fix the situation. If you were Jeff, what would you say? Also, if you were Barbara, how would you respond to Jeff's explanation?

4. How should Barbara and Jeff have handled this situation if they could do it over?

5. Use your library or the Internet to find information related to the theft of e-mail information or deliberate misuse of data found in electronic files. Report your findings to the class.

PROJECT: MY BUSINESS, INC.

Every business, even a very small one, is regulated and taxed by government. Regulations and taxes harm business people most often when they are not aware of them or do not understand them. In this chapter, you will study the effects of local, state, and federal laws on your business.

DATA COLLECTION

1. Identify the city/county office you will need to contact about:
   a. local zoning regulations
   b. licenses and permits
   c. taxes and fees

2. Identify an information source on the legal procedures necessary to start a new business. If your city or state has a booklet describing those procedures, obtain a copy. If you are able to identify a Web site that contains this information, record the URL or bookmark it so you can return to the site.

ANALYSIS

1. Analyze the information you collected in the Data Collection section above. Outline the legal procedures you would have to follow and identify the permits and licenses you would need to start your juice bar. List the problems you might have in adhering to the legal requirements.

2. The legislature in your state has just increased the sales tax from 4 percent to 6 percent of total sales. This will cause you problems because of the way you have priced your products. In order to make prices easier to remember and to simplify making change, you priced your products as shown below to include the 4 percent tax. (Do not be concerned if these are not the same products or prices you have previously identified for your juice bar.)

Large one-variety juice/yogurt mix	$3.75
Small 3-juice combo	$2.50
Vitamin/mineral supplement	$ .60
Turkey sandwich	$5.25
Bagel with cream cheese	$1.25
Nutrition bar	$1.90

It will be difficult to collect the additional 2 percent for sales tax and keep your pricing method. How will the sales tax increase affect your business? Evaluate several methods for dealing with the tax increase. Define your new pricing structure.

3. To reduce your startup costs and to find a business location with a large number of potential customers, you have decided to rent a mobile cart in a large local mall in which to start your juice bar. Many fast-food business owners in your city are concerned that if mobile carts are allowed to operate, they will take business away from the other restaurants. They have approached the city council to pass a zoning regulation to prevent food from being sold from mobile carts, suggesting that it might be a health hazard. What actions can you and the owners of other similar businesses take to prevent the zoning law from being adopted by the city council? If the law is passed, how will it affect your business?

4. Most businesses develop a unique name with a design or symbol to clearly identify the business for customers. They can then apply for a copyright or trademark to protect its use. Use a computer graphics program, if possible, to develop the name and symbol you will use for your business.

UNIT THREE

INFORMATION and COMMUNICATION SYSTEMS

CHAPTERS

Already, the Web work style is changing business processes at Microsoft and other companies. Replacing paper processes with collaborative digital processes has cut weeks out of our budgeting and other operational processes. Groups of people are using electronic tools to act together almost as fast as a single person could act, but with the insights of the entire team. Highly motivated teams are getting the benefit of everyone's thinking. With faster access to information about our sales, our partner activities, and most important, our customers, we are able to react faster to problems and opportunities.

Bill Gates
Business@ the Speed of Thought, 2000

TECHNOLOGY AND INFORMATION MANAGEMENT

OBJECTIVES

8-1 Describe basic elements of computers and the Internet.

8-2 Explain the chief information officer's role in managing an organization's computer systems and its electronic networks.

8-3 Describe information systems that managers use to aid in their decision making.

8-4 Discuss types of problems that employees face when working in today's high-technology organizations.

8-5 Describe technology's present and future impact on today's businesses.

BRAVE NEW BUSINESS WORLD

fter Mia Herrera rose, dressed, and hopped into her car, she used her voice-activated cell phone to call several customers who had e-mailed her late last evening. Before entering her favorite coffee shop, she reached into her pocket for her handheld computer and jotted a few brief messages that were then e-mailed to her regional sales manager. After enjoying breakfast and returning to the car, Mia opened her briefcase and was soon dictating a message on her computer that was sent wirelessly via the Internet to her office assistant. Before starting the

engine, she checked her car's global positioning system for the most direct but timesaving route to her new client.

At the next two stoplights, she read a few e-mails and found a favorite Web site to check yesterday's closing stock price for Egloff and Fox, Inc. Her first client that morning was the E&F purchasing manager. After reaching the parking lot, Mia quickly reviewed E&F's background and database files from the small wireless computer kept in her briefcase. Now she felt ready to face the business day ahead.

Through the ages, discoveries and inventions have had major impacts on society. No inventions in recent years have had a greater impact than the computer, Internet, World Wide Web, and wireless communications. These new tools have profoundly affected the personal work lives of Mia Herrera and millions of other workers. New technologies have made dizzying changes in the way we live and work, and the pace of change is not likely slow in the years ahead.

The traditional business office that once operated with filing cabinets, typewriters, and secretaries was labor intensive when compared to today's electronic office. Simple business transactions that once took weeks of paper handling are now processed in minutes. Now workers create and store most documents electronically.

Whether an office is in a bank, factory, or day-care center, it must still collect, process, store, retrieve, and distribute data. The modern electronic office is an information center operated by **knowledge workers**—people who work with information. Clerks,

FACTS AND FIGURES

In 1997, the Census Bureau surveyed the U.S. population to assess ownership and use of computers. Among the findings: More than one in three American households had computers. Almost three quarters of children used a computer at home or at school. Nearly half of American adults used a computer at home, work, or school. One in five Americans used the Internet.

ILLUSTRATION 8-1

How have new technologies changed the traditional business office?

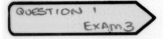

QUESTION 1
EXAM 3

supervisors, and managers at all levels are knowledge workers who handle data and information. **Data** are the original facts and figures that businesses generate, while **information** is data that have been processed in some meaningful way that is useful to decision makers.

In this chapter you will learn how technology has changed the way businesses handle data and information. You will also learn how computers and the Internet affect organizations, people, and jobs. Finally, you will learn how information systems help managers make sound decisions by getting the right information in the right form at the right time to the right people.

■ELECTRONIC TECHNOLOGY FUNDAMENTALS

The current electronic revolution started with the creation of the computer over 50 years ago. More recently the Internet developed into a tool that people and businesses could use to communicate with each other. The computer and the Internet plus additional electronic devices set the stage for reconstructing how businesses operate.

■ COMPUTERS

A **computer** is a machine that processes and stores data according to instructions stored in it. The machine parts and anything attached to it are called **hardware.** The instructions that tell the computer what to do are called **software**.

As illustrated in Figure 8-1, computers have three basic elements: a way to enter data, a central processing unit to act on the data, and a way to output the results. Users can enter data through such devices as keyboards, voice-recognition systems, and scanners. The central processing unit receives and processes the data as directed by the software stored permanently or temporarily in the computer. Users can view data entered and processed on monitors or can print or store the data on disks, such as hard drives, floppy disks, CDs (compact disks), and DVDs (digital video disks).

TYPES OF COMPUTERS Computers come in different sizes and serve different purposes. Companies use large computers (mainframes) to store and retrieve vast amounts of data for the entire company. Major divisions of the company may use medium-sized computers. The typical office computer that most workers use is a desktop or personal computer (PC). Workers can carry smaller computers (laptops or notebooks), such as those used by Mia Herrera in the opening story, in briefcases and backpacks.

In addition to desktops and laptops, smaller handheld devices also serve specific purposes. A **personal digital assistant (PDA)** is a computer-like device that can be carried in a pocket and used to, among other things, send and receive messages wirelessly. PDAs may also be built into cell phones. PDAs usually contain a calculator, an address

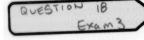

QUESTION 1B
Exam 3

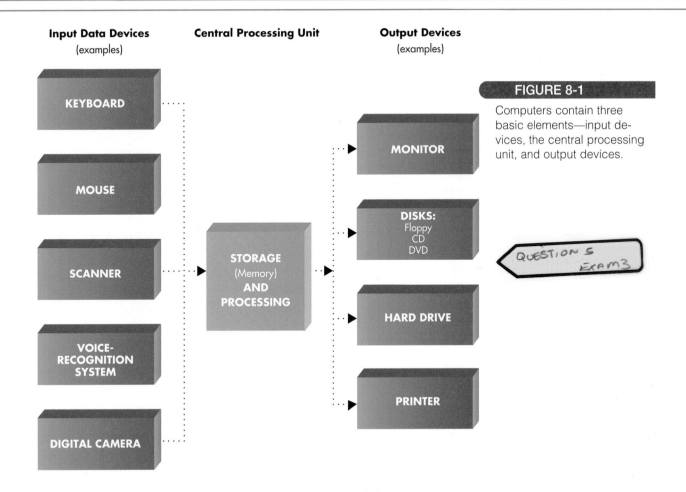

Input Data Devices (examples)

Central Processing Unit

Output Devices (examples)

KEYBOARD

MOUSE

SCANNER

VOICE-RECOGNITION SYSTEM

DIGITAL CAMERA

STORAGE (Memory) AND PROCESSING

MONITOR

DISKS: Floppy CD DVD

HARD DRIVE

PRINTER

QUESTION 5 EXAM 3

FIGURE 8-1

Computers contain three basic elements—input devices, the central processing unit, and output devices.

book, a notepad for keeping "to do" lists, and a fax modem. PDAs come with features to meet a variety of needs. Such devices will become standard voice-messaging equipment built into vehicles. Because wireless computing is rapidly developing, new products will continue to pour into the marketplace.

TYPES OF SOFTWARE All computers need two types software: operating system software and application software. **Operating system software** is a master control program that manages the computer's internal functions and file system. Operating system software directs and channels application software instructions and data for processing. Examples of operating system software include Microsoft Windows, MacOS, Unix, and Linux.

Application software refers to programs that perform specific tasks. The most common examples of application software are word processing for creating written documents, a spreadsheet for performing calculations on rows and columns of data, a database for storing related information for later retrieval, and software for creating graphics. A description of common business application software appears in Figure 8-2. Figure 8-3 shows an example of a spreadsheet. Many other types

TYPE AND APPLICATION

FIGURE 8-2

Other Common Types of Software Application Programs

ACCOUNTING

Maintain general and specific accounting records such as accounts receivable, accounts payable, and general ledger.

COMMUNICATIONS

Send and receive information from other computers, including fax, e-mail, and surfing the Web.

DESKTOP PUBLISHING

Create high-quality newsletters, brochures, manuals, advertising, and other special documents combining text, photographs, and graphics.

FORMS

Provide standard business forms such as invoices and purchase orders but allow for the modification of forms and the creation of entirely new forms.

GRAPHICS

Prepare diagrams, organization charts, line and bar graphs, pie charts, and other kinds of illustrations.

TRAINING

Teach employees about various topics, including how to use computers, how to supervise workers, and how to prepare a talk.

UTILITIES

Aid other software to work more effectively, such as providing a variety of type styles and font sizes, recovering lost files, and finding and correcting computer system errors.

Cartright Corporation Comparative Income Statements

FIGURE 8-3

Spreadsheets are used to prepare financial statements and other documents.

	Year 1	Year 2	Percent of Change
Sales	$58,000,000	$59,000,000	1.7
Cost of Goods Sold	30,000,000	32,000,000	6.7
Gross Profit on Sales	28,000,000	27,000,000	-3.6
Operating Expenses	12,000,000	11,000,000	-8.3
Administrative Expenses	10,000,000	9,000,000	-1.0
Net Profit Before Taxes	6,000,000	7,000,000	16.7

of popular software are available to perform specialized tasks. Companies, for example, produce sophisticated software packages that help businesses manage complex tasks, such as customer and supplier relationships.

MOORE'S LAW Advances in computer technology occur at an ever-increasing rate. An engineer named Gordon Moore of Intel Corporation predicted that the amount of data that could be processed by a computer chip would double about every 18 months. **Moore's Law,** as this prediction has become known, has proven to be rather accurate. Figure 8-4 shows this accelerating pace of change over the past two decades. According to Moore's Law, a computer bought only one to two years ago will be obsolete this year. As processing speed increases, high-tech companies are constantly producing new and better software to take advantage of the technology's capabilities.

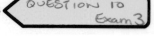

But new technologies make old equipment obsolete. Buying and installing new equipment and software, as well as re-training employees, are costly business expenditures.

■ THE INTERNET

Advances in computer technology invited the entrance of another electronic wonder—the Internet. The **Internet,** or **Net,** is a worldwide network of linked computers that allows users to transfer data and information from one computer to another anywhere in the world. People can use the Net to send e-mail, visit Web sites, and participate in discussion groups.

The Internet permits businesses to work together electronically and for employees to communicate with other employees at any distance. Even consumers can buy online from businesses or sell personal products. Two individuals with common interests can chat or join a discussion group, seek information from electronic libraries, or compare

The Development of Microprocessors

MICROPROCESSOR	TRANSISTORS	TOP SPEED	YEAR
8086	29,000	10 Megahertz	1978
80386DX	275,000	16 Megahertz	1985
Pentium	1,200,000	25 Megahertz	1993
Pentium III	9,500,000	733 Megahertz	1999

Source: *Modified from Business Week, November 15, 1999*

FIGURE 8-4

Microprocessors composed of chips on integrated circuits are constantly being developed by Intel Corporation and other firms to process data at faster speeds.

CAREER CONNECTION

WEBMASTER

Webmasters are called the "guardians of cyberspace." They are the people who create, organize, and manage Web sites for schools, businesses, and governmental organizations. There are two kinds of Webmasters: those who focus on hardware, software, and communication protocols (such as "http"), and those who focus on the site's content.

Every Webmaster needs to know the basics of the hardware that links computers to the Internet, the software the Internet uses, and the specialized languages and programming commands required to make the World Wide Web function, such as HTML, Java, JavaScript, and VRML. Thus, Webmasters spend their time in a highly technical environment that is constantly changing.

Webmasters often have access to many kinds of sensitive information and restricted files. On some sites, the Webmaster may also maintain the e-mail system. Therefore, issues of ethics and confidentiality may frequently arise.

Qualified Webmasters for major companies can demand large salaries, but working hours are often long. Much of the work may have to be done at night, when users are less likely to be using their computers.

For more career information about Webmasters, check your library or the Internet for resources.

products. The Internet is also used as a substitute for phoning and to download music and update computer software. Internet uses are virtually unlimited.

WORLD WIDE WEB Creation of the **World Wide Web, WWW,** or **Web** made the Internet accessible to the average person. Previously, the Internet allowed computer users to share only printed text and required sophisticated technical knowledge to use. Therefore, at first, researchers and the military were the main users. Now the Web permits text plus photographs, videos, and sound to be transmitted over the Net, all with just a minimal amount of computer savvy. This Internet access tool for the general public enabled the Net to grow rapidly during the last decade. Now, for most of us, the Web is synonymous with the Internet.

The Web uses links, called hyperlinks, for navigating easily among its pages. A **hyperlink** is a Web page address embedded in a word, phrase, or graphic that, when clicked, transports users to that address. Web pages usually contain hyperlinks to other sites on the Web that contain information of interest to site visitors. Hyperlinks often appear as colored, underscored words, but addresses can be embedded just about anywhere on the Web page. As you move your mouse pointer around a Web page, you will know when you encounter a hyperlink, because the pointer will turn to a hand with a pointing index finger.

Many companies, large and small, have Web sites. Their addresses usually contain the company name or initials. For example, the General Electric site address is http://www.ge.com. All addresses begin with "http://" for "hypertext transport protocol," which is a code that helps computers connect to each other on the Web. Your browser will assume that all addresses begin with this, so you need not type it. The next part of the address, www, stands for "World Wide Web." Many Web addresses begin this way, but not all. The company name or abbreviation usually appears next. The three letters at the end identify the type of organization. The ".com" follow-

QUESTION 17
Exam 3

ing "ge" indicates a commercial or profit-making organization. A government office is ".gov," a school is ".edu," and a not-for-profit organization is ".org." Saying "dot.com" is a way advertisers and others may refer to Web sites in general.

The line under the GE Web address shown above indicates a hyperlink. If you were reading this page on the Internet and you wanted to visit GE's home page, you could immediately jump there by clicking the mouse on the hyperlink. You may want to

QUESTION 11 Exam 3

know what products GE sells or what jobs are available. You could find out about GE's products by following hyperlinks on the company's site to different product pages.

Much business is transacted on the Internet. The use of the letter "e" before a name means "electronic." For example, "e-commerce" refers to businesses that buy and sell to other businesses as well as to businesses that sell to consumers. "E-business" means businesses that buy and sell only to other businesses. Retailers that sell to customers on the Web are known as "e-tailers." Anyone who sends messages to others is using "e-mail." And "e-appliances" are consumer appliances, such as refrigerators and microwave ovens, that contain chips allowing people to use e-mail to obtain data such as cooking, freezing, and maintenance information that can be stored in the e-appliance. New "e" words are likely to evolve. You will learn more about e-commerce in Chapter 9.

USING THE INTERNET To get onto the Internet, you need a **modem,** an electronic device inside or outside the computer that enables it to send data over phone lines or cable. You also need an **Internet Service Provider,** or **ISP,** a service that provides access to the Internet through its large computers. Examples of ISPs include AOL, Mindspring, and AT&T WorldNet. ISPs usually charge a monthly fee, but you can get free Internet access through Web-based services such as Juno and NetZero. Advertising pays for these services.

QUESTION 14 Exam 3

To use the Web, you also need a **browser.** This is a program that permits you to navigate and view Web pages. Most computers come

BUSINESS INNOVATION

THE NET'S BOOSTER ROCKET—THE WEB

The purpose of the first crude Internet was as an emergency communication system for the military in case an enemy attack knocked out more conventional means of communication. Soon after this important goal was achieved, experts began using the slow, unreliable, and troublesome military Internet to share research findings. At the same time, improvements were being made, but the system's clumsiness and the need for technical knowledge limited its growth. However, the stage was set for the next breakthrough.

In 1989, Tim Berners-Lee, an English physicist who had been working at the European Particle Physics Laboratory, created the World Wide Web. This relatively unknown Web inventor developed a means for using the Internet to send more than just typed material to any computer in the world. Needed was a global Internet-based hypermedia means for sharing global information. His new system permitted multimedia—graphics, videos, animations, and sounds—to be sent over the Internet. The Net's popularity began growing by leaps and bounds as further refinements were made. This laboratory also created the first Web browser, leading to navigation through hyperlinks. The marriage of the Internet and the Web led to rapid global acceptance during the 20th century's last decade.

Tim Berners-Lee believes the Web is a powerful force for social and economic change and that it has already modified how we conduct business, entertain ourselves, find information, and swap ideas. His goal is to keep the Web wide open and free to everyone, but he expects the Web will continue to alter our lives. He resisted efforts by major corporations to own and operate parts of the Web, because that would lead to charging user fees, which would not make it free. As the director of the World Wide Web Consortium, Berners-Lee discusses Web refinements with other consortium members worldwide. The group also oversees and recommends solutions to a variety of problems.

Tim Berners-Lee could have easily become very rich if he had personally built his own Web business or worked closely with a major computer firm to exploit it. He chooses to guide his creation to most benefit humankind. *Time* magazine named him one of the greatest geniuses of the 20th century. Yet, he is not a household name like Albert Einstein. But unlike many other famous people before him, he has a Web site.

THINK CRITICALLY

1. Why was the first Internet created? And why didn't the early version of the Internet catch on with everyone?
2. How did the addition of the WWW increase use of the Internet?
3. Do you think Tim Berners-Lee would be happier being the CEO of a highly successful firm making millions than he is now as an employee in nonprofit organizations?
4. Using a library or the Internet, find out more about Tim Berners-Lee and write a report for the class.

already equipped with a browser, or your ISP will provide one. The two most popular browsers are Microsoft Internet Explorer and Netscape Navigator.

Once you are on the Net, you can go directly to a Web address or you may have to search for information. A **search engine** is a program that assists in locating information on the Net. After you type in one or more key words, the search engine will display a list of sites that contain information matching those key words. Some of these sites may have the information you want, while others may be way off target. A mouse click will take you to the Web sites that look promising. For example, assume you wish to buy a notebook computer. To use a search engine such as Excite (www.excite.com), key in "notebook computer" and wait for Excite to provide a list of Web sites that you could visit.

■ MANAGING TECHNOLOGY

As computers became a dominant force throughout the world, organizations had to manage the computer systems as well as the computer specialists. In major organizations, the top computer executive is the **chief information officer,** or **CIO.** The CIO reports to the CEO (chief executive officer). The CIO not only must have knowledge about electronic equipment but must also possess expert management skills.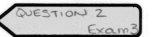

QUESTION 2
Exam 3

CIOs must keep up with new technologies and know what types of equipment to purchase to meet an organization's specific needs. Because many workers use computers, keeping employees trained and productive is equally important. CIOs make it possible for all people who need information to get it easily and quickly from anywhere it exists. CIOs also protect information from being improperly used or getting to people who should not have it.

■ DISTRIBUTING INFORMATION

Employees are constantly using their computers to record, process, send, store, and retrieve information. The company's computer system must make these tasks easy and fast to perform. **Telecommunications (data communications)** is the movement of information from one location to another location electronically. The means used for this movement may be telephone lines, cable, or satellite. Telecommunications companies sell different systems for transmitting information within firms and to business partners and customers. Customers can even have training programs and sports events appear on a portion of their computer monitors, thanks to telecommunication providers.

Workers need an electronic means for sharing information. A **local area network (LAN)** is a network of linked computers that serves users in a single building or building complex. In a LAN, a computer that stores data and application software for all PC workstations is called a **file server,** or, more commonly, a **server.**

QUESTION 20
Exam 3

Firms with multiple locations have to send information to employees who are geographically dispersed. A **wide area network (WAN)** is a network of linked computers that covers a wide geographic area, such as a state or country. The LANs and the WANs and their servers are connected to a mainframe computer. The servers are also channels through which individual workers can use their computers to communicate with others inside and outside the organization.

■ INTRANETS AND EXTRANETS

An **intranet** is a private company network that allows employees to share resources no matter where they are located. An intranet works like the Internet. Users access information through a browser, navigate with hyperlinks, and send e-mail through the intranet. Usually the intranet even connects to the Internet, but it is sealed off from the general public to protect company information.

Intranets enable employees to accomplish many electronic tasks. Groups of employees working on the same project can discuss, share, plan, and implement ideas without having to leave their desks. These same employees can use company records stored electronically to aid in performing their tasks. Workers may use their computers to check employer-sponsored events, such as new training programs, or see choices of health care benefits and the balance in their retirement plan. The easy accessibility of information on an intranet reduces the time spent finding and thumbing through paper documents.

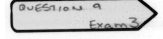

Another type of network that operates similar to the Internet is an extranet. An **extranet** is a private network that companies use to share certain information with selected people outside the organization, such as suppliers and major customers. A supplier of raw materials for a manufacturer or merchandise for a national retailer, for instance, could serve the company better by tracking the company's daily inventory balance. When inventory gets low, the supplier could deliver its goods just when the company needs them. An extranet can enable the supplier to see the company's inventory records without allowing access to other company data.

■ INFORMATION SECURITY

One of the major concerns of chief information officers is information security. The CIO must do whatever is necessary to make certain that hackers cannot steal, destroy, or alter information. The penalty for not controlling information may well be lawsuits by employees, customers, suppliers, and the public, as well as the loss of critical company records.

Organizations also may violate business ethics when they gather, and sometimes sell, information about people who use the Internet to browse or buy merchandise. Programs launched from Web sites can track your travels from Web site to Web site. Where you go frequently on the Web reveals your general interests and what you buy. After collecting this information, some firms may sell it to businesses that sell goods related to your interests. For example, if you frequently look at Web sites related to MP3 music or games, firms that sell these goods will contact you and try to sell you their products.

When you buy goods on the Net, you must provide basic information, such as name, address, telephone number, and e-mail address. Often Web sites store this information in your computer as a "cookie" file that the sites can retrieve when you visit again. This can be helpful when you buy from the business again. But the seller can also sell this personal information to other businesses without your knowledge.

The Federal Trade Commission and good business practice require that businesses notify buyers of their rights and how personal information will be used. However, some businesses may not properly inform buyers of their rights or continue to sell their confidential information. These actions are unethical and illegal in some states. Many computer users would buy on the Internet if they did not fear invasion of their privacy.

Companies must also take defensive strategies to protect electronic information. Such strategies often include requiring user passwords to access data, saving information as backup files, and scrambling information to make it unreadable to others.

Firms often use firewall systems to protect information from outsiders who try to break into their networks. A **firewall** uses special software that screens people who enter and/or exit a network by requesting specific information such as passwords. Passwords should change frequently. But even firewalls are not totally hacker proof. Other systems are either available or being developed. For example, fingerprints, voice verifica-

FACTS AND FIGURES

Businesses involved in e-commerce are advised to have a privacy policy, post it on their Web site, and make it well known. Companies should: give notice about what personal information is collected and how it is used; give consumers the choice about whether and how their information can be used; establish adequate security measures to provide data protection; and allow consumers to access the data about them, so they can attest to its accuracy and make changes if necessary.

ILLUSTRATION 8-3

Why is information security such a critical issue? What are some ways in which information can be protected?

tion, retina scanning, and other methods are being tested to safeguard organizational information.

■ INFORMATION SYSTEMS

Organizations are experiencing an information explosion. New computerized methods can gather and store more information quickly than could traditional methods. As a result, many managers suffer from information overload, the existence of more data than anyone can attend to. Information overload leads to needless costs and inefficiencies, as managers try to sort through all the available information to find what they really need to make decisions. Thus, organizations need effective means for managing information.

Employees generate business data constantly. They record sales transactions, collect customer information, and track inventory. When employees key such data into their computers, the data become part of the company's database. A **database** is a collection of data organized in a way that makes the data easy to find, update, and manage.

But a collection of data is not useful until it is processed into a form that decision makers can use. A computer system that processes data into meaningful information is called an **information system.** Three key types of information systems are management information systems, decision support systems, and executive information systems.

■ MANAGEMENT INFORMATION SYSTEM

A **management information system (MIS)** is an information system that integrates data from various departments to make it available to help managers with day-to-day business operations. An MIS deals with specific and highly structured data. Different departments collect and process the data. Employees enter daily transactions into the system as they occur, such as when they prepare purchase orders and record sales. From this gathered and stored information, managers can request reports to help them make daily operating decisions. For example, a sales report can show a manager where sales are slow. From this information, the manager might decide to do a special promotion for customers in this area.

■ DECISION SUPPORT SYSTEM

A **decision support system (DSS)** is a system that helps managers consider alternatives in making specific decisions. For example, a DSS can help a manager determine the most efficient routes for the company's delivery trucks. The ability to analyze "what if?" scenarios is a key capability of a DSS. *What if* we continue our current strategy? Would that work? *What if* we try something else? What are the likely consequences of that action? The company's management information system provides much of the information for its decision support system.

■ EXECUTIVE INFORMATION SYSTEM

An **executive information system (EIS)** combines and summarizes ongoing transactions within the company to provide top-level executives with information needed to make decisions affecting the present and future goals and direction of an organization. Information used in executive information systems is gathered from the MIS and DSS. An EIS collects data from both internal and external sources to help executives make decisions. For example, executives might use the EIS to collect outside information that affects the company, such as information regarding competitors, the state of the economy, and government policies. With information from inside and outside the organization, top managers make long-term decisions that help a business survive and grow.

■ THE EFFECTS OF TECHNOLOGY ON WORK AND WORKERS

Computers, the Internet, and other forms of electronic technology have affected our lives as consumers and as workers. The work of employees has changed because of new technological devices and because firms have restructured the ways in which they operate. Over the last several decades, computers have changed the way individuals perform work tasks, which in turn has caused anxieties in people about job security, about their ability to cope with new technology, and about electronic devices that may affect their health.

■ HEALTH PROBLEMS

Certain complaints arise among workers who spend most of their work time using computers and other automated equipment. Employees may complain about eyestrain, cancer-causing radiation, backaches, and hand-muscle problems. Eyestrain is likely to occur when computer operators view monitors (computer screens) for long periods. Usually, eyestrain can be reduced or eliminated by adjusting light intensity on screens, shading screens from glare, wearing glare-reducing glasses, and taking work breaks every few hours. Sitting in uncomfortable chairs for long periods can cause back problems. Hand problems are often the result of improper keyboard or chair heights. Proper chair design with good back support helps, as do special exercise routines and breaks from being seated for long periods.

Employees may also be concerned about radiation. Many types of electronic equipment such as cell phones, televisions, and computers give off modest amounts of radiation. Some studies have shown that the amount of radiation is small and therefore does not affect health. However, other studies claim computer radiation is harmful. Pregnant women are especially concerned. Many businesses assign women to non-computer jobs during pregnancy to avoid possible harm from radiation.

What health problems can occur when computers are used frequently? What steps can a business take to reduce such problems?

QUESTION 7
Exam 3

The science of adapting equipment to the work and health needs of people is called **ergonomics.** Ergonomic experts study the relationships between people and machines. For example, they work with engineers to design more comfortable chairs and to produce lighting that reduces eyestrain. In recent years, ergonomic experts have been spending much time making computer hardware, software, furniture, and lights adjustable, practical, and comfortable.

■ CHANGED JOBS

A major role of today's managers is to manage change. The rapid rate at which changes occur can be disruptive. To survive, businesses must be adaptable and employees must change to meet the needs of employers.

Nearly all jobs have been restructured, and new jobs are evolving. Large numbers of employees need to use computers. In turn, job tasks once done manually, such as using shorthand and typewriters, are now done on computers. Bosses who key their own messages have greatly modified the role of the secretary. For example, most secretaries have had title changes, with many becoming administrative assistants performing a variety of higher-level tasks. Many are assigned leadership roles, serve as project managers and members of work teams, and train employees on how to use electronic equipment. Similarly, other jobs have been greatly modified, with workers having far more responsibilities than during the pre-computer age.

Often employees are retrained for new jobs, but others are let go. This downsizing action creates anxiety among workers. While many firms help employees get retrained, some firms help employees find new jobs with other firms. Each new major technological change, however, creates employee anxiety. Managers must be ready to deal with this problem, because these employees may become less productive, leave, or create problems.

THE NEW JOB MARKET

Computerization has caused a reduction in the need for some skills and increased need for other skills. Today's employees must have technical skills as well as interpersonal skills. For example, employees who work at computer help desks give assistance to workers who have computer problems. Help desk employees must have "people skills," such as a friendly personality and a willingness to help others. They must also have a great deal of technical knowledge about computers and about solving software problems that employees encounter.

Other technically oriented jobs include programmer (one who creates and modifies software programs); network administrator; systems analyst (one who helps create and develop and maintain MIS, DSS, and EIS); software trainer; Web page designer; Webmaster (someone who manages and maintains a Web site); computer equipment salesperson; and computer repair person.

Telecommuters, as mentioned in Chapter 2, work at home using electronic equipment such as computers, scanners, and printers to complete their "at home" tasks. Still other individuals are entrepreneurs who start and run their own businesses from home using electronic equipment. Many of the popular Internet businesses were started from the homes of entrepreneurs.

THE FUTURE

Computer technology is now an indispensable part of business throughout the world. Businesses either move with the technology or fade away. Well-managed firms do not stand still. How much additional change will occur during the next five to ten years? No one knows, because these are dynamic times. What is known, however, is that change is constant and is occurring at amazing speeds. Rapid change has been occurring in nearly every industry and in most countries. Slow-moving firms are attempting to catch up. Some of those are catching up by buying healthy firms or are creating joint ventures that will propel them into the 21st century.

The world is in the middle of a major shift in how to conduct business. Just as cars, planes, television, and telephones changed life during the last century, the computer is changing life in this century. It is transforming how we work and live. One of the biggest change agents in this age of transformation is the Internet. It has increased the intensity of worldwide competition. No longer can major businesses in any nation think of their markets or competitors being exclusively within their own boundaries.

Computer scientists, computer engineers, and systems analysts are expected to be the three fastest growing occupations through the year 2006. The increase will be driven by the very rapid expansion in computer and data processing services, which is projected to be the fastest growing industry.

The cost of producing goods and services in this electronic age has led to increased competition that has lowered prices. And computers and other electric marvels have cut paperwork, increased worker productivity, shed non-productive tasks, and maximized business efficiency. Consumers have been the beneficiaries. Even the nature of how businesses are organized and operated have been permanently affected. This Internet age, however, does not mean that all firms have closed their doors where customers might enter to see, touch, and even try before they purchase. You cannot go to a health club or a hairstylist on the Internet, but you can get advice there. You may prefer to go to the grocery store for the personal contact. But in this fast-paced world, you may prefer to buy your groceries on the Internet and have them delivered to you.

Many businesses will thrive by operating stores on Main Street and on the Internet. Like Mia Herrera in the opening story, we will have our personal digital assistants as we meet and talk with friends from our homes and cars, in restaurants, and at the mall.

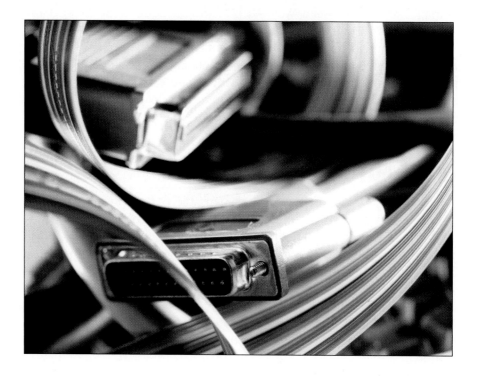

CHAPTER CONCEPTS

■ Computers come in all sizes, shapes, and configurations, and all need an operating system and application software to perform tasks. Advances in technology require computer systems and software to be updated often.

■ The Internet is a worldwide network of linked computers that permits users to share data and information freely and quickly over phone lines or cable. The development of the World Wide Web made the Internet accessible to the non-technical general public through a Web browser and hyperlink navigation.

■ The chief information officer is accountable for managing all of an organization's electronic information and supporting systems that help managers and other employees make timely and informed decisions. CIOs are responsible for keeping electronic systems up to date, safeguarding data, and making information available to managers in a form they can use to make decisions.

■ Many businesses have management information systems (MIS), decision support systems (DSS), and executive information systems (ESS). An MIS integrates data from many departments, making it available to managers for day-to-day decisions. A DSS helps managers consider alternatives in making specific decisions by using "what if?" scenarios to predict results of different actions. An ESS combines and summarizes ongoing transactions within the company to help top-level managers make decisions affecting the future direction of the company.

■ Computers have modified existing jobs and created new jobs. Employees have been affected in various ways, including new job and skill requirements, layoff fears, and health factors.

■ The electronic world will continue to undergo vast changes. Business must adapt to technological advancements to survive.

BUILD VOCABULARY POWER

Define the following terms and concepts.

1. knowledge workers
2. data
3. information
4. computer
5. hardware
6. software
7. personal digital assistant (PDA)
8. operating system software
9. application software
10. Moore's law
11. Internet (Net)
12. World Wide Web (WWW or Web)
13. hyperlink
14. modem
15. internet service provider (ISP)
16. browser
17. search engine
18. chief information officer (CIO)
19. telecommunications (data communications)

20. local area network (LAN)
21. file server (server)
22. wide area network (WAN)
23. intranet
24. extranet
25. firewall
26. database
27. information system
28. management information system (MIS)
29. decision support system (DSS)
30. executive information system (EIS)
31. ergonomics

REVIEW FACTS

1. What are the three elements of a computer?
2. How does application software differ from operating system software?
3. What does Moore's Law predict about the computer equipment a company buys today?
4. How does the Internet differ from the World Wide Web?
5. What two things do you typically need in order to connect to the Internet?
6. What are the two main characteristics that a chief information officer must possess to be successful?
7. How does a LAN differ from a WAN?
8. Why does a CIO need to be concerned about information security?
9. What new ways are being tried to make sure that the wrong people do not gain entrance to information on a firm's computer system?
10. What kinds of data go into a management information system, and how do they get in the system?
11. How does a decision support system help managers make decisions?
12. Name three types of jobs that are available in the computer field.
13. From what kinds of electronic equipment might radiation cause damage to one's health?
14. Who have been the primary beneficiaries of the efficiencies that have resulted from the use of electronic technology by businesses?

DISCUSS IDEAS

1. How does an older type of business office differ from a computerized business office?
2. What type of employee would need a personal digital assistant at work?
3. What implications might Moore's Law have on the chief financial officer's job?
4. Assume you are exchanging ideas using e-mail with a friend. Your friend keyed "www.hp.com" and suggested it as a source of information for your next class report. What does the keyed-in information represent?

5. Using one or more search engines, find a master list of search engines. Report your results to the class.

6. How has the development of the World Wide Web made the Internet accessible to the average person?

7. How does an intranet differ from an extranet, and how do these networks relate to the Internet?

8. Assume you work for a large business with lots of computerized equipment. It has branches in five American cities and seven foreign countries. The branches need to share information. What might you require in terms of servers and information systems?

9. You have been made an ergonomics expert at your school. Identify ergonomic problems and propose changes that would protect the health of students, teachers, and other employees.

10. The desks at XYZ Company had no keyboard trays. Computer keyboards were just placed on desks. After consultation with ergonomics experts, the company installed adjustable trays under the desks. Discuss the benefits of this change on employee wellness, productivity, and morale.

ANALYZE INFORMATION

1. Deborah and Kenneth Parks obtained prices from the following companies for a desktop computer system with a modem for their new business.

	Computer House	EZ-Electronics
Computer	$1,200	$1,000
Monitor	500	550
Fax	300	275
Printer	400	350
Software programs	850	950

   a. Which company has the best total price and by how much?

   b. If the Parkses purchased each item from the company with the lowest price, what would their total cost be? How much would they pay each company?

2. The Parkses want to use the Internet to buy merchandise from suppliers and to set up a Web page for selling their goods. They checked the service reliability, quality, and monthly rates from three Internet service providers. Firm A charges $30, is nationally known, provides the first month of service free, and is disabled by hackers once or twice a month but is back up and running within an hour or two. Firm B charges $25 and is national but not well known. It offers no free-use time and is disabled infrequently; however, it offers outstanding assistance when users have questions or problems. Firm C charges $18, is much smaller, has never been disabled, offers no free-use time, and its help line is not especially good. What firm should the Parkses select? Explain.

3. The Onyx Corporation estimates it spends $50,000 annually to process data by using its traditional methods and equipment. A proposed computer system would cost $150,000 for equipment, software, and installation. In addition to depreciating the equipment at the rate of $30,000 per year, the company would spend $24,000 annually to process data.

   a. During the first year after installing the new computer, would it cost more or less to process data? By how much?

   b. How many years will it take to fully depreciate the equipment?

   c. What will it cost to operate the computer system during the sixth year?

   d. If the computer system is installed and lasts seven years, how much will Onyx spend in total for the computer system and how much will be saved or lost?

4. With instructions from your teacher, join other students to identify and analyze the types of computer problems your group has had. Include in your report any trouble group members have had with losing data and files from school or home computers on or off the Internet. Prepare a report to your class about the problems and indicate the security steps that should be taken to prevent or reduce these problems from happening.

5. Using a library or the Internet, find information about a specific ergonomic problem related to working with electronic equipment, such as one related to radiation from computer equipment, uncomfortable chairs, or poorly designed desks. Prepare a report of your findings.

SOLVE BUSINESS PROBLEMS

CASE 8-1

Carmen Alonso and Mary Ann Corsi were on their lunch break at work when a friend, Jan Bailey, joined them. In due time, each person expressed her concerns about trying to juggle home life with work, raising a family, and spending time with others. "It's a crazy world," Jan said. "No wonder everyone tries to keep up by being glued to cell phones." Carmen was concerned that cell phones cause accidents. Mary Ann added that she spent much time at home ordering things from the Internet. "There's almost no time for the mall or to grocery shop, let alone to spend quality time with the children." At that point, Jan launched the heated conversation that follows:

Jan: *The world has gone overboard with all this electronic technology. Yes, we use the phones and e-mail to chat with family and friends, but that's not the same as seeing people in person.*

Mary Ann: *That's better than not having cell phones or the Internet. I think these gadgets are aids, not obstacles. How else could we both work if we couldn't stay in touch, even if it's not in person?*

Carmen: *Communication is too impersonal these days, too cold. Everyone's rushing to get things done. Few people stop to have an old-fashioned conversation. I wish we could turn the calendars back 25 years when people just sat around and chatted.*

Mary Ann: *But you wouldn't have all the luxuries we have today. You'd be wasting time chatting. The Internet allows you to get so much more done. I'll bet my parents would have loved to have what we have.*

Carmen: *Mine refuse to learn to use the new technology. They're very happy without the gadgets.*

Jan: *I agree with Carmen's parents sometimes. We have new problems, like worrying about someone stealing our personal records, destroying our files, and crashing our computers. Those can be expensive problems in terms of time, money, and invasion of privacy.*

Think Critically:

1. Design a simple set of questions that you could ask people about the advantages and disadvantages of having much new technology to use away from work. Ask your parents, grandparents, or other similarly aged adults to answer your questions and to comment on life today versus the past, when computers may not have made much of an impact. Prepare a report for your class.

2. Do you tend to agree more with Jan, Mary Ann, or Carmen? Explain why you feel the way you do. Which person most likes and which most dislikes today's technological times?

3. Answer these questions about yourself:
   a. What electronic equipment such as cell phones, computers, access to the Internet, scanners, digital cameras, or other devices do you personally have readily available to you seven days a week?
   b. Which one piece of electronic equipment is *most* valuable and which is *least* valuable to you? Explain why.
   c. If you had the money to buy one additional new piece of electronic equipment, what would it be and how would it benefit you in terms of school or work?

4. Use your library or the Internet to find information that deals with the topic of how electronic equipment contributes to the possible depersonalization of everyday life. Report the results to your class.

CASE 8-2

Ai-ling Shen and Jack Compton are both employed at the Waterside Company, a small life insurance firm. Both Ai-ling and Jack have been with the business for over ten years but are now quite upset by recent events. The office manager announced yesterday that all employees must attend several all-day training sessions on two forthcoming changes. A new computer system is replacing the old one, and jobs are being restructured to improve processes that will lead to greater efficiencies and enhanced productivity.

Unlike past practice, the new plan will have each person in the office doing all of the tasks now done separately. The training will prepare them to do everyone else's work, but all work will be done on the computer. To even the workload, all ten standard insurance policies will be loaded in each computer, and employees and salespersons will be assigned specific customers on an alphabetic basis. Then, when a salesperson calls with questions, the designated office worker can find the answers immediately. With the old system, answers might take as long as two weeks to get to customers.

The new computerized system has been installed but will not be used until the employees are all trained. They have just returned from the first day's training session. The following conversation takes place:

Jack: *I don't know about you, Ai-ling, but this change is just like coming to an entirely new job. I don't know how all of this is going to work out.*

Ai-ling: *We should have at least been told about this in advance, rather than have it come as a complete surprise. We could easily get a job at another insurance company. Maybe we should quit. The company isn't willing to give us more money to learn all the new procedures, new software, and new computers. With our experience, we shouldn't have any trouble finding a new job.*

Jack: *Hold on, Ai-ling. We shouldn't be too hasty. We make good money here. I agree, however, that they should have told us about this so we could have been doing some reading and getting ourselves ready for the change. If the system works well, our jobs will be more secure. Most other insurance companies already operate the new way.*

Ai-ling: *From what we learned today, we could certainly make the company sorry that they didn't get our opinions before deciding to change computers and our jobs.*

Think Critically:

1. Describe what mistake the Waterside Company management made in replacing the computer system.
2. In what ways could Ai-ling make the company regret not involving the employees in the decision? Explain.
3. If the new computer system is to be successful, will it be because of restructuring the work, installing a new computer system, or both? Explain your answer.
4. If the new changes are successful, how will the salespeople and customers benefit?

PROJECT: MY BUSINESS, INC.

As the owner of a new business, you will spend a great deal of time dealing with information. Poorly organized business records would make it hard for you to find and use the information you need. Use the following activities to review information management systems for small businesses and make decisions about how technology will benefit your business.

DATA COLLECTION

1. Interview an owner of a small business. Discuss the type of information management system used in that business. Identify (a) the type of records and information maintained, (b) whether or not the system is computer based, (c) who is responsible for information management, and (d) how the system could be improved.
2. Visit a computer systems retailer and discuss the hardware and software the retailer recommends for new small businesses. Collect information on system prices, capabilities, and ease of operation.
3. Visit an office furniture company in person or online and investigate ways to create an ergonomically healthy work environment for your employees.

4. Using the Yellow Pages or the Internet, identify businesses that offer information management services for businesses. Contact one company and determine the types of services offered and prices charged for those services.

ANALYSIS

1. The Internet can be a very valuable tool for small businesses. Identify and describe five specific types of information, accessible through the Internet, that can help you develop and manage your business. Then use an Internet search engine to identify one or more sites that supply each type of information you listed. Bookmark each location (use a diskette to store your bookmarks) so you can easily revisit the sites.
2. List three ways that e-commerce might have a negative effect on your business and three ways that you might use e-commerce to improve your new business.

E-COMMERCE

OBJECTIVES

9-1 Describe the recent growth of the Internet.

9-2 Discuss common business uses of the Internet besides selling products.

9-3 Describe the stages businesses commonly go through in developing an e-commerce business.

9-4 Identify successful e-commerce businesses and strategies.

9-5 Outline the steps for starting a new e-commerce business.

THE CASE FOR CYBER COMMERCE

uran Ozmat sat in the Chamber of Commerce meeting only half-listening to the presentation. The speaker was talking about the use of the Internet by businesses. She had just made the statement that any business without a presence on the Web would be at a competitive disadvantage in the next few years.

Turan thought of his photography studio and believed the speaker couldn't be talking about that type of business. His business required personal contact between the photographer and the customer. Customers wanted to be able to come into the studio and see the quality of the portraits and photos as well as the settings and backgrounds that Turan used. Whether people were scheduling a wedding, family portraits, or students' graduation photos, Turan believed that face-to-face meetings always allowed him to un-

derstand the customer's needs and to develop the customer's trust and confidence. He didn't see how any of that could be possible with the Internet.

When Turan returned to his business that afternoon, he still was thinking about the speaker's comments. Even though he felt his business was different, he didn't want to miss an opportunity. He sat down at his computer, typed "photographer" into a search engine, and was amazed at the results. The search engine returned over 100,000 hits! Turan narrowed the search by typing in the name of his city. Immediately, three of his competitors' business names popped on the screen. Turan decided he would spend the weekend exploring how other photography businesses were using the Internet.

People are sitting down at their computers in ever-increasing numbers to use the Internet. Sometimes it is hard to believe that the Internet has a relatively short history. It developed from the first efforts to link computers less than 50 years ago. The introduction of the personal computer in the late 1970s began to expand computer access onto business desktops and into homes. Today, through low-cost or free connections to the Internet, millions of people throughout the world can instantly access information and communicate with each other.

The Internet has become a very important business tool. **E-commerce** means doing business online. It includes the use of the Internet to buy and sell products as well as exchange business-related information, such as transmitting purchase orders electronically or advertising online. E-commerce is now a multi-billion-dollar part of our economy.

The Internet has allowed many small businesses to compete with larger, established companies and to reach consumers all over the world. While currently less than 1 percent of all business sales are completed using the Internet, that figure is growing rapidly. Businesses need to plan for e-commerce.

■ THE GROWTH OF THE INTERNET

Since its infancy as a military and research tool in the 1950s, the Internet has grown impressively, as shown in Figure 9-1. Over 10,000,000 Web

E-commerce experts believe that there is a tremendous amount of money to be made in online business-to-business selling. They attribute this to the fact that selling to businesses is more cost effective than to individual consumers; orders from businesses are, on the average, higher in dollar value; and businesses order larger quantities of an item.

sites were available at the end of the 1900s, with millions more being added each year. Since the invention of the World Wide Web in the late 1960s, access to the Internet has grown to an estimated 500 million people around the world. Almost 50 million homes in the U.S. had access to the Internet in 2000, up from just 13 million in 1995. The U.S. leads the world in Internet use, with approximately 40 percent of all users. However, Internet users are found all over the world, as shown in Figure 9-2.

Business use of the Internet is increasing rapidly as well. While there are many other business uses of the Internet, as we will discuss in the next section, an important measure of business Internet use is the sale of products and services. According to the U.S. Department of Commerce, U.S. Internet sales to consumers in 1998 totaled $8 billion. That seems like a very large figure, until it is compared to the business-to-business Internet sales in the same year. Business-to-business (B2B) sales totaled $45 billion. Still, there is a great deal of room for growth in the Internet sale of products and services. The total sales to consumers represent less than 1 percent of all consumer purchases. Internet sales worldwide are expected to reach two trillion dollars by 2005, with nearly 200 million regular Internet customers. Some experts say even that estimate is low.

FIGURE 9-1

The Growth of the Internet

Year	1970	1980	1990	2000
Estimated number of Web site providers	4	200	300,000	10,000,000

Source: *U.S. Department of Commerce*

RANK	COUNTRY	% OF USERS
1	United States	42.9%
2	Japan	6.9%
3	United Kingdom	5.4%
4	Canada	5.1%
5	Germany	4.7%
6	Australia	2.7%
7	Brazil	2.6%
8	China	2.4%
9	France	2.2%
10	South Korea	2.2%

FIGURE 9-2

Countries with the Most Internet Users in 2000

QUESTION 4 Exam 3

Source: *Computer Industry Almanac*

■ BUSINESS USES OF THE INTERNET

In the opening scenario, Turan didn't believe the Internet was useful for his photography business. Like many of us, he was considering only the ways he could sell his products using the Web and not the many other uses of the Internet. While the use of the Internet for selling products is important, businesses can benefit from this new tool in many other ways. Those uses include communications, information gathering, and improving business operations.

■ BUSINESS COMMUNICATIONS

Businesses use the Internet most for communication, both within and outside the company. Most internal communications on the Internet are completed using e-mail. But new tools are available to assist with communications, including videophones and software that allows several people to share application software and collaborate using text and graphics tools while sitting at their computers. Using the Internet, a company can post an employee newsletter online. This speeds the information to all employees while reducing the mailing and distribution costs. Employees can quickly send reports, memos,

ILLUSTRATION 9-2

For what purpose do businesses use the Internet most frequently?

and other information to co-workers.

Companies use the Internet to communicate with current and potential customers. The Internet has become an important way to provide information about the company and its products to customers. Remember in the chapter-opening story that when Turan was searching for information on photographers, he quickly located the Web sites of three of his local competitors. As customers try to locate specific products and businesses, they are increasingly turning to the Internet. Even those who use telephone directories to identify businesses often want more information than is typically included in a directory advertisement. By using the Internet, a customer can often obtain product descriptions, determine the days and hours a business is open, and even print a map showing the location of the business. Today, if a business has not posted information about its business, location, and products and services on the Internet, it will likely miss some customers.

Businesses also communicate with each other using the Internet. Business people send e-mail messages, exchange documents, and sell their company's products and services to other businesses. Common business-to-business services offered via the Internet include online training, financial planning and accounting, maintaining personnel records, and data processing.

■ INFORMATION GATHERING

A second business use of the Internet is for research. You have probably used the Internet to gather information for a project or report. Businesses also use the Internet to obtain information they need in order to make decisions. A great deal of information on the Internet is free and is provided by government agencies, colleges and universities, libraries, and even private businesses. Other information that businesses need can be purchased from companies specializing in research, from professional and trade associations, and from publishers. For example, Dun & Bradstreet provides specialized research reports, information, and publications for businesses.

Businesses can also gather information on current and prospective customers. When companies sell products, they often encourage purchasers to complete a product registration or warranty online. People who regularly use the Internet are more likely to complete a product registration if it is online than if they have to fill in a registration card by hand and mail it. The registration process allows the company to collect important information about the customer, including address, telephone number, and even an e-mail address. That information is valuable in future communications and promotional activities with customers. Also, the company can gather information on where the product was purchased, the price, reasons for purchasing the product, and other related products the consumer currently owns or plans to purchase.

Many Web sites include a place where prospective customers can request information, be placed on an e-mail or mailing list, or obtain answers to specific questions. That capability allows the company to develop a list of prospective customers and determine their specific interests. The information can be used for future communications and promotions.

Competitive information is easier to obtain using the Internet. A great deal of information is contained in many businesses' Web pages. It is relatively easy to learn about the competitors' products, prices, credit terms, distribution policies, and the types of customer services offered. Some Web sites provide information on product tests, offer comparisons and reviews of products, and even have places for consumers to discuss their experiences with a company and its products.

CYBER COMMUNICATION

Because of the simplicity involved in sending and receiving e-mail, many messages are brief and casual. However, in a business setting, e-mail should be used with care. Your managers and colleagues will use your messages to judge your on-the-job performance. Don't send messages just because you can.

In business, e-mail is generally used in the following ways:

- To provide a record of certain events that have occurred or specific things that have been said.
- To advise supervisors or peers on particular topics or procedures.
- To direct others to do something specific.
- To state company policy and explain procedures.
- To pass on information.
- To promote goodwill.

ACTIVITY Look at the list above that shows how e-mail can be used in business circumstances. Select one of the situations, and describe—verbally or in writing—a possible scenario that would fit that situation. For example, as a supervisor, you might send an e-mail to an employee, directing that person to call a vendor about an undelivered shipment of merchandise.

IMPROVING BUSINESS OPERATIONS

The Internet has become an important tool to improve business operations and control costs. Salespeople can log on to the company's Web site and determine whether a certain product is in inventory for delivery to a customer. When a product is sold, the order can immediately be entered into the computer from anywhere in the world to speed the processing and shipping of the order. A production manager can access the records of a transportation company to see when an expected shipment of raw materials will be delivered. An accountant in a branch office can download financial statements from the main computer to compare current financial performance with last year's information. Product designers from three countries can collaborate on a new design by examining a three-dimensional drawing online and making changes that each of them can see instantly.

Small businesses can benefit competitively from the use of the Internet due to the rapid exchange of information. For example, several small automotive parts retailers can consolidate their orders through an e-business wholesaler by submitting information on needed parts via the Internet. Then the wholesaler can place a very large order with the manufacturer and receive a significant price reduction for each of the retailers. This can be done almost instantly with online order processing. In addition to the lower costs, the needed parts get to the retailers quickly, rather than taking days and weeks under older purchasing methods.

The Internet has proven to be an important tool in reducing the cost of several business activities. A recent government report identified the following cost savings to businesses when customers used the Internet:

Ordering airline tickets	87% savings
Online banking	89% savings
Paying bills	67% savings
Distributing software	99% savings

■ STAGES OF E-COMMERCE DEVELOPMENT

A company that does almost all of its business activities through the Internet is often referred to as a **dot-com business.** The name "dot com" comes from the end of a commercial business's Web address: *.com*. While a growing number of dot-com companies have received a great deal of publicity (Amazon.com, Priceline.com, Ameritrade.com), most businesses use the Internet for only a portion of their activities. Businesses that complete most of their business activities at a physical location rather than through the Internet are referred to as **bricks-and-mortar businesses.** The name "bricks-and-mortar" suggests that the company conducts most of its business in an actual building.

Businesses generally progress through three stages as they develop their e-commerce presence on the Internet: (1) They begin by offering information only. (2) Then they progress to interactive capabilities and finally (3) to full integration of business transactions on the Web. Figure 9-3 summarizes these stages.

■ INFORMATION STAGE

Most existing businesses first begin using the Internet for e-commerce by developing a basic Web site. The site often is quite simple—only one or a very few pages. It provides basic information about the company that might typically be included in an advertisement or brochure. Customers can use the Web site when trying to locate information about where they can purchase specific products and to learn more about the

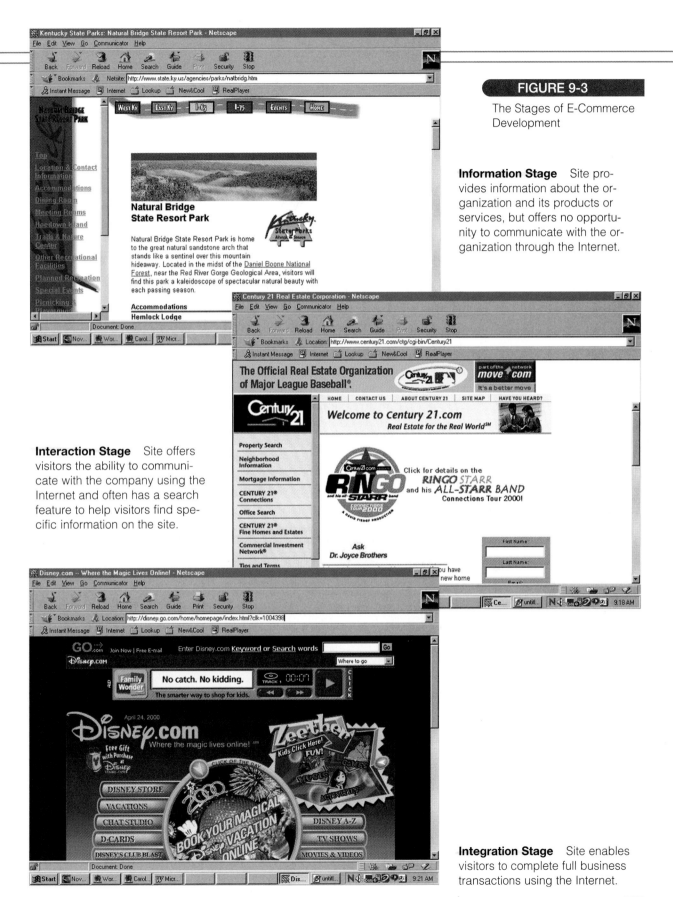

FIGURE 9-3

The Stages of E-Commerce Development

Information Stage Site provides information about the organization and its products or services, but offers no opportunity to communicate with the organization through the Internet.

Interaction Stage Site offers visitors the ability to communicate with the company using the Internet and often has a search feature to help visitors find specific information on the site.

Integration Stage Site enables visitors to complete full business transactions using the Internet.

company and its products. As the company gains more experience with the Internet, it will add additional information with *hyperlinks* (also called *links*) from the home page. The company might add complete product descriptions, information on payment methods, customer services, and even product manuals, updates, and procedures for obtaining product upgrades.

The limitation of the first stage of e-commerce development is that customers cannot use the Web site to interact with the business. They must still visit the business in person or use the telephone, mail, or other traditional methods to obtain information that is not on the Web site or to make a purchase.

■ INTERACTION STAGE

The second stage of e-commerce development is interaction. In addition to providing information, the site offers visitors the ability to interact with the company using the Web site. The first type of interaction is the use of e-mail. Site visitors click a link to bring up an e-mail form that they can use to request information, ask questions, or contact specific people in the company.

Beyond e-mail, companies can add a database, where customers can search for specific information, such as choices of brands, product features, and services. They can check product availability, calculate product costs and shipping charges, and determine how long it will take to have an order delivered. There may even be three-dimensional photos, short video clips, or simple models of products for customers to examine.

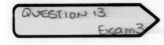

It is possible with interactive e-commerce for customers to place orders using information from the Web site, but not place the orders directly from the site. An order form may be included on the site along with a product catalog. Customers can complete, print, and then fax or mail the form to the company.

■ INTEGRATION STAGE

Companies that want to take full advantage of the Internet in their business move to full integration. With full integration, the entire customer transaction can be completed using the Internet. Customers can get necessary product, pricing, and shipping information. They can place an order and pay for the order, track their shipment until it is delivered, and obtain customer assistance following the sale—all using the Internet. Companies with integrated business activities do not have to be dot-com companies. Much of their business can still be accomplished through traditional methods. But customers will be able to complete their business transactions with the company using the Internet if they choose.

Consider how Turan Ozmot can begin to use the Internet in his photography business. Since competitors are already using the Internet, he should at least develop a Web page and advertise on the Web in order to make prospective customers aware of his business and the services he offers. He could include examples of his photos and portraits on the Web site. As Turan gains more experience with the Internet, he may find ways to build customer interaction into the site. Turan may choose not to have a fully integrated Web site, but he may be able to sell some types of products online, such as reprints of photos and related products such as frames and photo albums.

ILLUSTRATION 9-3

What does it mean if a company has a fully integrated e-commerce presence on the Internet?

■ SUCCESS WITH E-COMMERCE

Although e-commerce is still very young, it has already had a major impact on the way business is done. New types of businesses have appeared, offering products and services that did not exist prior to the Internet. Web design companies, Internet service providers (ISPs), and Web security businesses are some of these new types of businesses.

Web-based business activities have resulted in many new kinds of jobs as well. Today, you can become a Webmaster or Web applications developer, which wasn't possible just a few years ago. In 1999, over 2 million people worked in jobs directly related to the development and management of Internet operations in companies. Nearly 1 million more worked in positions that support companies' new e-commerce activities.

Companies such as Dell Computer Corporation and Charles Schwab investment brokerage company have emerged as industry leaders as a result of their moves into e-commerce. New companies including Amazon.com, eBay.com, and Buy.com have formed in order to take advantage of this new type of business activities.

■ LEADING INTERNET BUSINESSES

As you learned earlier, consumers currently purchase billions of dollars of products over the Internet each year. Customers are more likely to purchase certain types of products online than others. The top Internet retailers for 1999 are listed in Figure 9-4. As you can see, books, computer hardware and software, and music are the most frequently purchased items.

While most of the companies on the list sell computer hardware and software, several well-known bricks-and-mortar companies have moved

FIGURE 9-4

Top Internet Retailers in 1999

WEB SITE	TYPE OF BUSINESS	ESTIMATED ANNUAL SALES
Ebay.com	Online auctions	$1.3 billion
Amazon.com	Bookstore	1.1 billion
Dell.com	Computer manufacturer	600 million
Buy.com	Consumer electronics	400 million
OnSale.com	Computers & software	350 million
Gateway.com	Computer manufacturer	300 million
Egghead.com	Computers & software	200 million
Barnesandnoble.com	Books and CDs	175 million
CDNow.com	CDs and movies	175 million
AOL.com	Varied merchandise	150 million

Source: *Stores magazine*

into the top 20 of Internet retailers. They include The Gap, Lands' End, and Wal-Mart. Other rapidly growing product categories for consumer purchases on the Internet are travel, investing, insurance, and toys.

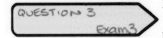

QUESTION 3
Exam 3

In business-to-business Internet sales, computers and electronics have the highest sales volume, as they do in consumer sales. The other top categories in business sales are utilities (electricity and gas), petroleum and chemicals, vehicles, office supplies, and shipping services.

Another rapidly growing area of Internet sales is advertising. In 1998, businesses spent less than 2 billion dollars to advertise their products and services on the Internet. By 2003, that figure is expected to grow to $15 billion or more. Among the top Internet advertisers are Microsoft, Amazon.com, Yahoo!, Barnes and Noble, and E*Trade. Some advertising costs are hidden, since many small Internet businesses use bartering to place their ads on another Web site. In return, they run advertisements for the cooperating businesses on their Web site. No money is exchanged between the companies to pay for the advertising.

You have probably noticed when you go online that the Internet is filled with advertisements. Since space on a Web page is limited, companies compete for the attention of Internet users. They will try to place their advertisements on pages that prospective customers are most likely to visit. They also use creative advertising designs. Varied sizes, colors, and placements of advertisements encourage Internet users to stop and read the company's information. Advertisements now include moving text and graphics plus links to more detailed information.

The Internet Advertising Bureau has established standards for the size and appearance of Internet advertisements. Internet advertising is measured in pixels. A **pixel,** short for PIX (picture) ELement, is one or more dots that act as the smallest unit on a video display screen. Some of the common sizes of Internet ads are illustrated in Figure 9-5.

■ MEETING CUSTOMER NEEDS

E-commerce is still a very new method of conducting business for both companies and consumers. As with anything new, only a small percentage of businesses and consumers are willing to try the Internet. From the successes and failures of the first e-commerce efforts, we can learn how to be more successful.

FIGURE 9-5

Sizes of Common Internet Advertisements

Full Banner 468 x 60 pixels

Half Banner 234 x 60 pixels

Button 120 x 90 pixels

**Micro Button
88 x 31 pixels**

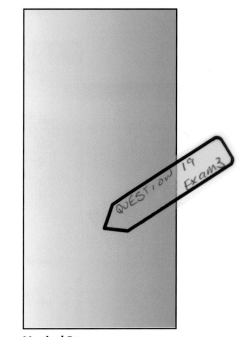

**Vertical Banner
120 x 240 pixels**

Most people today are not using the Internet to purchase products. In fact, only 2 percent of Internet users say they go online with the specific intention to make a purchase. Over 80 percent say their primary reason for going online is communication. If they are interested in purchasing products, consumers are more likely to use the Internet to gather information and to compare alternatives. Then many will go to a local business to make the purchase.

The primary reasons consumers report that they do not shop online are security concerns, difficulty in making purchases using the Internet, and a belief that they will receive poor customer service if there are problems with the order or the product. To be successful with e-commerce, businesses must create Web sites that move customers from information-gathering to making a purchase. Customers will need to have confidence that the shopping experience will be positive and trouble free.

Online shoppers are often very loyal to specific businesses and brands. They usually prefer to shop at the same businesses and buy the same brands that they have traditionally purchased. However, they will switch to other businesses and brands if the online shopping experience is not satisfactory. Consumers list the following factors as important in maintaining their loyalty to an e-commerce business:

1. An understandable, easy-to-use Web site
2. Getting products quickly after ordering them
3. Familiar businesses and brand names
4. Useful and accurate information

On the other hand, the factors that will cause customers to switch to another company for their online purchases are:

ILLUSTRATION 9-4

What are some reasons why consumers might be loyal to particular e-commerce businesses?

1. Out-of-date or limited information
2. Slow response time in answering questions, processing orders, and shipping merchandise
3. A Web site that is very slow or frequently does not work
4. Poor customer service

Advertising, careful pricing, and even online coupons are proving to be important in encouraging consumers to try online buying. Most important, however, is an inviting, easy-to-use Web site with effective customer service. If consumers have a bad experience with a company's online sales, it is very difficult to get them to come back. Consumers say that low prices and special offers will not influence them to use an online business again if they have had a bad shopping experience.

Because of the growth of the Internet and e-commerce, many organizations have begun to identify the best Web page designs and most effective online business sites. The Webby Awards were developed by the International Academy of Digital Arts and Sciences to recognize the best Web sites each year. This association presents awards in a large number of categories, including "commerce," which identifies the best business uses of the Web. Experts select one set of awards, and consumers vote on another set.

QUESTION 6
Exam 3

Sales copy on a business's Web site should be short and to the point. Paragraphs should be limited to fewer than 10 lines each. Use bulleted lists, indented paragraphs, bold or colored type, and other devices to break up copy.

■ ESTABLISHING AN E-COMMERCE BUSINESS

Developing an effective e-business requires careful planning. It is not easy to get people to buy from an online business, especially if it is a new business with which customers are not familiar. Large businesses invest millions of dollars in creating and managing their Internet operations. Small businesses can create attractive, professional-looking Web sites themselves for much less, using commercially available Web authoring software. Whether businesses create their sites themselves or hire professional Web designers to do it, they must still carefully plan the design and content of their site, and update it regularly to keep customers coming back.

If you own a small business and want to establish an e-commerce Web site, you should follow these steps to help insure its success:

1. Determine the purpose of your Web site.
2. Study your customers, their needs, and their Internet experience.
3. Plan your online business.
4. Obtain a Web server and domain name.

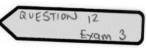

QUESTION 12
Exam 3

5. Develop order processing and customer service procedures.
6. Design the Web site.
7. Advertise your online business.
8. Open for business.

DETERMINE THE PURPOSE OF YOUR WEB SITE

You may want to have your entire business on the Internet or you may want to use it only to promote your bricks-and-mortar business and provide information to prospective customers. Some products and services are easier to sell over the Internet than others. Study the sites of similar businesses and talk to experts in e-commerce to determine whether to use the Internet for a limited set of business activities at first and progress gradually toward full integration, or limit your goals for your site to the informational or interactive stage.

STUDY YOUR CUSTOMERS

To develop an online business that your customers will use, you must first know who your customers are, what they want, and their interest in doing business online. You will want to know their experience with e-commerce and whether they use the Internet primarily for information or for shopping. What products do they typically buy online, and which are they more likely to buy from a bricks-and-mortar business? The ages of prospective customers are important as well. Younger consumers are often more comfortable with the use of computers, while older shoppers may be reluctant to purchase online. You need to understand your customers in order to design a Web site that is inviting to them and gives them confidence to purchase from your business.

PLAN YOUR ONLINE BUSINESS

Based on your study, you will determine what products and services to offer through your online business and whether you will have an information-only, interactive, or integrated Web site. If your entire business is not going to be online, you must determine where and how the bricks-and-mortar part of your business will operate.

Another decision is whether you will complete all activities yourself or use other businesses for some of them. For example, most e-commerce businesses use transportation companies such as FedEx or UPS to ship their merchandise. Others use banks or other financial institutions to process credit card transactions and collect payment from customers.

OBTAIN A SERVER AND DOMAIN NAME

An Internet business relies on computer technology for operations. In Chapter 8, you learned about servers—computers that contain the software and store the data for networks. A Web server is the backbone of an e-commerce business. In addition to the server, the Internet site must be easily accessible to a number of customers at one time, any time of the day. If customers cannot access the Web site whenever they want or if it has technical problems, they will not return to your online business.

Because many new and small businesses do not have adequate computer or network technology or do not have the needed technical skills to build and manage a Web site, they use a Web-hosting service. A **Web-hosting service** is a private business that maintains the Web sites of individuals and organizations on its computers for a fee. The Web-hosting service often provides design services, the hardware and software needed to maintain Web sites, and the technical personnel to make sure the Web sites operate effectively.

To open your Web business, you will need an Internet address to locate your site. A Web-site owner's unique Internet address is its **domain name.** Most Internet addresses for businesses use the following format—www.*businessname*.com. Before you can use a domain name, you must register it with one of several companies that maintain and approve all domain names used throughout the world. Registration currently costs $35 per year. Many possible domain names have already been registered, so you may not get your first choice. Also, individuals have registered many popular names and specific words related to products and services, hoping they can sell the domain name at a sizeable profit to a business wanting to use that name.

DEVELOP ORDER PROCESSING AND PROCEDURES

If your business will process orders and collect payments online, you will need specialized software. Many companies offer software that enables the use of **electronic shopping carts.** These are specialized programs that keep track of shoppers' selections as they shop, provide an order form for them to complete, and submit the form to the company through the Internet.

Also, you will need a secure server to accept credit card payments while protecting your customers' personal data from theft. Your business will need a process to quickly check the customers' credit and approve credit card purchases. You will also want to offer customers the alternative of paying by check if they are not comfortable with using a credit card online.

After the order has been accepted, you will need a process for quickly and accurately filling the order and delivering it to the customer. Also, customers will expect you to accept returns, replace products damaged in shipment, and offer other services to make sure their shopping experience is positive.

DESIGN THE WEB SITE

This step in developing an online business may seem to be out of order. Many people want to design their Web pages as the first step. However, until you plan the business completely, you will not know what needs to go on your Web site. Remember, to be successful, Web sites must be attractive and easy to use. If customers cannot find the information they need, if the site takes a long time to load, or if ordering instructions are confusing, prospective customers will leave your site and go to a competitor's business.

FACTS AND FIGURES

If consumers pay by credit or charge card online, their transactions are protected by the Fair Credit Billing Act. Under this law, consumers have the right to dispute charges under certain circumstances and temporarily withhold payment while the creditor is investigating them.

ETHICAL ISSUES

TAX FAIRNESS AND E-COMMERCE

Sales of products and services on the Internet have exceeded almost everyone's expectations. While e-commerce sales of both consumer products and business products are a very small percentage of the total sales of goods and services in the U.S., there is a mounting complaint from bricks-and-mortar retailers and from state and local government officials. The complaint—e-commerce companies are not currently required to collect sales taxes on the products they sell over the Internet, although some states require them to do so when they sell to customers within their home state.

Sales tax in most states is a small percentage of the cost of the purchase, usually 3-5 percent. So why should this tax matter to other businesses and to the government? Just look at the total amount of dollars spent on Internet purchases. When you total all of the purchases and apply the sales tax rate, it amounts to millions of dollars. State governments are missing out on those dollars that would help them balance their budgets.

Bricks-and-mortar businesses say it is unfair competition. Sales tax increases the price of products to customers. Traditional businesses believe that if e-commerce businesses don't have to collect sales tax from customers, they can sell their products for less, giving them an unfair advantage. Traditional businesses feel that if they must collect and pay the tax, e-commerce companies should as well.

On the other hand, e-commerce businesses say that customers already pay taxes for access to the Internet. Telephone companies and Internet Service Providers that provide connections to the Internet are required to collect federal and state taxes on their services. E-commerce companies also suggest that eliminating sales tax does not reduce the cost of products purchased online, since they charge shipping and handling costs that are much higher than the amount of the sales tax.

It would be very difficult for an Internet business to collect sales taxes imposed by each state and city. The tax rate would differ for each location and might change regularly. Each business would have to collect the correct amount of tax based on where the customer lives and then send the tax to the correct state or city.

THINK CRITICALLY

1. Currently in many states, some products (such as food and newspapers) are not subjected to sales tax while other products (such as automobiles and business equipment) have a lower sales tax rate. Do you agree that all businesses should be treated equally in the amount of taxes they are required to collect? Why or why not?
2. What effect, if any, do you believe it will have on Internet sales if e-businesses are required to collect sales taxes? Justify your answer.
3. Use the Internet to find recent information on the status of taxation of e-commerce sales by the federal government as well as by your state and city.

Web sites should use a basic design with easy-to-understand buttons and links. If customers can purchase products through the Web site, the shopping and ordering procedures should be very obvious and simple. Shoppers should be assured of security and customer service.

ILLUSTRATION 9-5

Why is designing a Web site not the first step in developing an online business?

■ ADVERTISE YOUR ONLINE BUSINESS

As with any new business, prospective customers will not know your online business exists without advertising and promotion. Two steps will help you promote your online business. First, register your business with the major search engines, such as Yahoo, Excite, AltaVista, and Infoseek. Each search engine has an electronic means for collecting site addresses and categorizing them by key words, so that Web visitors can find them. However, you can make sure the search engines include your site under appropriate key words by registering it with them directly. You can find registration information at the search engines sites.

The second step is to advertise and promote your e-commerce business. It is important to place advertising for your business in other Internet locations where prospective customers are likely to search for information related to the products and services you sell. You may want to sponsor sites that are popular with the people you would like to attract to your business. Make sure your Web address is included in all materials your business distributes and in all advertising you do.

FACTS AND FIGURES

Online entrepreneurs can ask themselves these questions when evaluating the shopping experience on their sites: Are there good pictures of all the products? Is ordering easy, and is the site navigation clear? Does the site look professional? Does the site offer something people can't get elsewhere?

■ OPEN FOR BUSINESS

After careful planning, you are now ready to open your Internet business. As with any business, you will have to maintain the Web site and update it regularly. You will want to keep in contact with customers to make sure they are pleased with your site and with their purchase experiences. Watch competitors to keep up-to-date with the products and services they are offering. Keep up with the latest technology and online business procedures to make sure your e-commerce business continues to be successful.

CHAPTER CONCEPTS

■ The Internet is growing rapidly, with over 500 million people worldwide who have access to the Internet and 10 million Web sites available at the end of the 1990s. Business is moving to the Internet as well. By 2000, online retail sales totaled over $8 billion dollars and business-to-business online sales topped $45 billion. Those figures are expected to increase dramatically each year.

■ Buying and selling merchandise is not the primary use of the Internet for either consumers or businesses. Consumers use the Internet most frequently for communications and to gather information. Businesses use the Internet to communicate internally and externally, to gather information about prospective customers and other businesses, and to improve business operations.

■ The growth of e-commerce has led to a number of new businesses and new jobs that would not exist without the Internet. Those jobs include the design and management of Web sites and the administration of Web security. Traditional businesses have also begun to use the Internet to advertise, to provide customer information, and even to buy and sell products and services.

■ Online customers will be loyal to businesses that have easy-to-use Web sites, provide shopping security, and offer efficient delivery and customer service. However, if customers have problems with an online business, they are likely to switch to a competitor or use a bricks-and-mortar business.

■ Planning your e-commerce business begins by determining how you want to use the Internet and studying your customers. With this information, you can then plan your online business. You will need special hardware and software to run your site and procedures for processing orders and delivering your products. Next, you must design and advertise your site. Finally, you are ready to open your e-commerce site for business.

BUILD VOCABULARY POWER

Define the following terms and concepts.

1. e-commerce
2. dot-com business
3. bricks-and-mortar business
4. pixel
5. Web-hosting service
6. domain name
7. electronic shopping carts

REVIEW FACTS

1. Was the approximate number of U.S. homes with access to the Internet in 2000 closer to 10 million or 50 million?
2. Are more consumer sales or business-to-business sales made using the Internet?
3. Are there more Internet users in the U.S. than in the rest of the world combined?

4. What other business activities are included in e-commerce besides buying and selling?

5. What are several common business-to-business services offered through the Internet?

6. How can businesses use the Internet to gather information on customers who have just purchased a product?

7. How did the name "dot-com" develop?

8. In which stage of e-commerce development do businesses make the least use of the Internet?

9. What are examples of types of businesses that did not exist prior to the development of the Internet?

10. Which types of products did consumers most frequently purchase using the Internet in 1999?

11. What are the names of several sizes of Internet advertisements?

12. What are the three primary reasons customers report that they do not shop online?

13. Why does an e-commerce business need a domain name?

DISCUSS IDEAS

1. Why does the Internet make it easier for small businesses to compete with larger businesses?

2. What are some possible reasons that the Internet sale of products and services is expected to grow very rapidly in the next several years?

3. Do you agree or disagree with the following statement: "Today, if a business has not posted information about its business, location, and products and services on the Internet, it will likely miss some customers." Justify your answer.

4. Why would private businesses choose to provide important information needed by other businesses free on the Internet rather than charging for it?

5. Why do you believe there are such large cost savings to businesses when they use the Internet to sell airline tickets, provide banking and bill-paying services, or distribute software?

6. What types of businesses do you believe are most likely to use the Internet only for information rather than developing interaction or integration? Why did you select those types of businesses?

7. What are some examples of effective and ineffective types of interaction you have seen on business Web sites?

8. Why do you believe most successful bricks-and-mortar companies are not among the top 20 Internet retailers?

9. Why do only a few Internet users go online to purchase products and services, while most go online to gather information and then purchase products from a local business?

10. If you owned a new e-commerce business that sold CDs and music videos, on what types of Internet sites would you advertise to make prospective customers aware of your business?

ANALYZE INFORMATION

1. A recent report showed the following past and projected growth in business-to-business Internet sales over a 5-year period:

Year	Total Sales
1998	$ 45 billion
1999	110 billion
2000	252 billion
2001	499 billion
2002	843 billion

Using those figures, calculate the following amounts:
a. the amount of increase in sales for each year
b. the percentage of increase in sales for each year
c. the total increase in sales for the 5-year period
d. the total percentage of increase in sales for the 5-year period
Using a computer graphing or spreadsheet program, prepare a bar graph illustrating the year-by-year growth in sales.

2. The use of the Internet varies, based on individuals' ethnic and racial background. The following chart illustrates the number of people in the U.S. based on major ethnic/racial classification and the percentage of that population that use the Internet.

Racial/Ethnic Classification	U.S. Adult Population (in millions)	Percentage of Population Using the Internet
African-Americans	4.9	28%
Hispanic	3.5	28%
All U.S. ethnic minorities	14.4	31%
Caucasian/White	52.8	37%

a. Calculate the number of Internet users for each racial/ethnic classification listed. Then determine the total of the U.S. adult population, the total number of Internet users in the U.S. adult population, and the average percentage of the total population using the Internet.
b. What are some possible reasons why the usage rate of the Internet varies, based on a person's racial/ethnic classification?

3. Go online and find at least three examples of businesses for each stage of e-commerce development: information, interaction, integration. If possible, print a copy of each company's home page. Using that home page, describe why the business fits the stage in which you classified it.

4. Go online and locate examples of advertisements that fit each of the types and sizes listed in Figure 9-5. Prepare an illustration of the advertisements you located by copying, saving, or printing the images or by drawing the ads on a sheet of paper. If you find other commonly used types and sizes of ads, add them to your illustration. Your teacher may ask you and other class members to develop a visual display of all of the illustrations or to make an oral presentation of your illustration.

5. Form a team with other class members. As a team, develop a list of at least five factors that everyone agrees makes an effective e-commerce business. Then, using the Internet and your list of factors, find several e-commerce businesses and rate them using the list of factors. You may want to have each student rate each business and then combine your ratings into a total team rating. Using your results, identify the best and worst e-commerce business. Share your results in a discussion with other teams in your class. Compare the factors your team identified with those of other teams and compare each team's choice of best and worst e-commerce businesses.

SOLVE BUSINESS PROBLEMS

CASE 9-1

Jillian and Dontae were sitting in front of the computer, listening to music they had downloaded and looking at a Web site that identified the top e-tailers for the year.

Jillian: *I really like the idea of shopping on the Web. It seems like you get many more choices, probably lower prices, and it's so convenient.*

Dontae: *I'm not sure I'm convinced yet. Look at the names of some of the businesses on the list. I've never heard of many of them. Do you believe they're all legitimate?*

Jillian: *Well, some of our favorite stores are on the list, so you could start with buying from them.*

Dontae: *But why not just go to the mall and buy from the stores? I'd get the products faster and not have to pay shipping charges. Besides, I don't want to enter my credit card number online, even if it says it's safe.*

Jillian: *But you hand your credit card to a person in every store when you make a purchase. They process it through a telephone line to get the amount approved. Isn't that the same thing?*

Think Critically:

1. Many people do not trust businesses that sell products online, especially if they are not familiar with the company's name. Yet they will walk into a new business in their city and shop without a great deal of concern. What causes the difference in people's view of online businesses compared to traditional businesses?

2. Do you agree with Dontae that it is easier to shop in an actual store in a mall than shop from the same business online? Why or why not?

3. What is your opinion of Jillian's comparison between entering a credit card number online and handing the card to a clerk in a business, who checks it using a telephone line from the store to the credit card company?

CASE 9-2

Jimmy Lai Chee-Ying is taking on two giants in Hong Kong. According to a report from CNN.com/ASIANOW, his new business venture uses the Internet as well as telephones and fax to take orders for grocery products. The orders are filled in eight warehouses located throughout the city and are delivered in one of 220 vans to the customer's home. He is taking on giants, since two supermarket chains control over 60 percent of the grocery business in Hong Kong.

Lai believes his business can be successful for two reasons. He offers a very limited selection of products. He carefully studies customer needs and sells the products they buy frequently and in larger quantities, such as soda pop, juice, canned goods, and baby diapers. He also selects products that he can offer for prices as much as 40 percent lower than the big supermarkets. And, he also sells computers. Why? Every home needs a computer, and if they buy a computer, they are more likely to purchase over the Internet.

Some business experts say he cannot succeed. People aren't willing to buy most of their groceries in a store and then order a few online. Others feel the larger stores will cut their prices and drive Lai out of business. But Lai looks at it differently. All customers like to save money with the convenience of home delivery. As he becomes more successful online, he can add more products. Because the two chains are so large, they will hardly notice the lost business resulting from the new e-business.

Think Critically:

1. Do you believe it was a good idea for Jimmy Lai Chee-Ying to start a new business that competes with two very large businesses that control most of the grocery market in Hong Kong? Justify your answer.
2. Discuss the advantages and disadvantages of Lai's strategy of selling a very limited number of popular products. What do you think of his idea for selling computers?
3. Why is the new e-business able to sell products at a much lower price than the larger chains? Do you believe the large businesses will drop their prices on the products Lai sells? Why or why not?
4. Identify another new Internet business that is competing with much larger traditional businesses. What is the business doing to encourage customers to switch from the larger business to the new e-business?

PROJECT: MY BUSINESS, INC.

E-commerce may allow new businesses to compete equally with larger, established businesses. Many businesses develop a simple Web site to provide information about the business, while others use the Internet more extensively. Some even complete all of their business online. Consider how you can use the Internet in your business.

DATA COLLECTION

1. Use the Internet to identify:
   a. Information sources that will be helpful in completing your business planning.
   b. Examples of other juice and beverage businesses that are using the Internet.
   c. E-commerce businesses from which you could purchase products and services you will use in your business.

2. Identify at least two Web-hosting companies that work with small businesses. Collect information on the services they provide and the costs of their services.
3. Conduct a short survey of 10 or more people who you believe would be prospective customers of your business.
   a. How regularly do they use the Internet and how much time per week do they spend online?
   b. Do they purchase products online? How regularly and what types of products?
   c. What are their positive and negative feelings about e-commerce and making purchases online?

ANALYSIS

1. Prepare a chart that compares the advantages and disadvantages of e-commerce for your business. Based on the chart, make a decision about whether you will use the Internet for your business: (a) right away, (b) after your business has operated for a few years, (c) probably not at all.
2. Outline the way you would use the Internet for your business if you used it for: (a) information, (b) interaction, and (c) integration.

3. Look at privacy statements on several Web sites. Then write one for your company. It should state the ethical guidelines you plan to follow in the online collection and use of customer data and in e-mail communications with them.

4. Using three of the Internet advertisement formats shown in Figure 9-5, develop advertisements you would use to encourage consumers to visit your business's Web site. Then go to the Internet and identify three sites that accept advertising you believe would be good locations for your ads. List the URL address for each site and give a brief rationale for each choice.

ORGANIZATIONAL COMMUNICATIONS

OBJECTIVES

10-1 Describe the communication process and channels.

10-2 Identify communication barriers and means for overcoming them.

10-3 Explain how corporate culture influences formal and informal communication networks.

10-4 Describe how to handle conflicts and how to run productive meetings.

10-5 Explain the types of communication problems that can occur when conducting business in foreign countries.

10-6 Identify ways to improve communications in organizations.

MANY WAYS TO COMMUNICATE

rica Komuro, one of many managers for an international book company, sat at her desk looking at tomorrow's schedule. In the morning, she would review the new organization chart for her department that would appear in the employees' manual. Later, she would meet with two other managers and her boss to resolve a conflict. She dreaded the shouting match that was sure to occur between two people who never agreed on anything.

The afternoon would include interviewing a new employee and giving her best worker instructions on how to perform a new assignment. Then Erica would write a few business letters and e-mail messages. She also had to finish her computerized monthly report for the division manager, which would be sent over the local area network. If the morning meeting did not

drag on, Erica might also have time to return phone calls that came in while she was dealing with a customer relations problem. Perhaps she could also squeeze in a call to Sabrina in Accounting to learn more about a rumor regarding the sudden resignation of the vice president.

Just before leaving the office she flipped the calendar page ahead a few days. In large letters she saw: "Meet with Mr. Nozaki." She was not sure how to best deal with the major problems this manager had in running the Tokyo office. At least she could recall a few Japanese words from earlier days when her family lived in Kyoto.

As she closed the office door, she smiled and waved to the evening cleaning person arriving for duty. On the way to her car she thought, "Tomorrow will be a busy day."

E rica is a typical manager because much of her time is spent communicating—speaking, listening, writing, and reading. Managers communicate in person, by phone and fax, by e-mail, and by paper documents. They also communicate through other means, such as a smile, a frown, or a wave.

Communications are vital in running organizations. Communications provide a link between employees and customers and between employees and managers. In fact, it has been estimated that managers communicate more than two thirds of each workday, as shown in Figure 10-1.

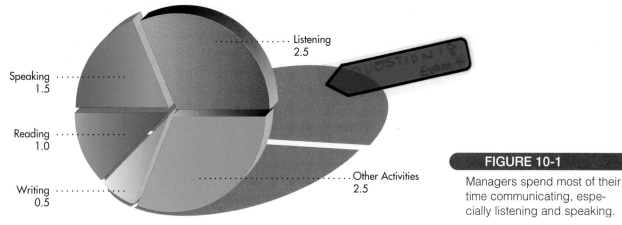

Speaking
1.5

Listening
2.5

Reading
1.0

Writing
0.5

Other Activities
2.5

FIGURE 10-1

Managers spend most of their time communicating, especially listening and speaking.

In this chapter you will learn about the communication process, corporate communications, and communication problems. You will also learn what good businesses and managers do to improve communications.

THE COMMUNICATION PROCESS

Communication is the sharing of information, in which the receiver understands the meaning of the message in the way the sender intended. Communication includes more than passing along factual data. It includes sharing ideas, beliefs, and opinions. It is a *two-way process* between senders and receivers. The senders must put the information into clear words, and the receivers must try to understand the message as the senders intended. If the receivers do not fully understand the message or need more information, they should ask for clarification. Thus, feedback is critical to effective communication.

Feedback is a receiver's response to a sender's message. The response may be in the form of asking questions to clarify the meaning of a message. Or, receivers may restate the message in their own words, so that the senders can verify that the receivers understood the meaning as intended. The communication process and the role of feedback are illustrated in Figure 10-2.

COMMUNICATION BARRIERS

The meaning of communication is simple to understand. Yet, poor communication is one of the biggest problems managers face. Poor communication can lead to disagreements, faulty work, delayed performances, and major industrial accidents. Two major barriers that interfere with communication are distractions and distortions.

FIGURE 10-2

The communication process involves a sender, a message, and a receiver. Feedback helps the sender and receiver make sure that both understand the meaning in the same way.

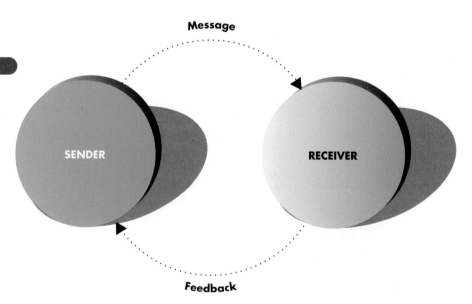

ILLUSTRATION 10-1

What kinds of distractions can occur during a business meeting? How can these barriers to communication be overcome?

DISTRACTIONS Interruptions occur all too often while communicating. Anything that interferes with the sender's creating and delivering a message and the receiver's getting and interpreting a message is a **distraction.** Distractions are potential causes of communication problems. Two workers who whisper to each other during a meeting create a distraction that may cause a nearby worker to miss a point made by the manager. It may also cause the manager to forget to mention a point. Ringing phones, grammar errors in messages, and loud noises are other examples of barriers to communications.

Because distractions affect communication, some managers learn to work with various interruptions, while others try to keep interruptions to a minimum. For example, some managers place telephone calls or write messages during specific times of the day when interruptions are less likely to occur.

DISTORTIONS When senders create messages, they must select the information they want to include. They need not include every bit of data surrounding an idea, event, or situation. Senders select only the information that they think the receivers need in order to understand the message. Depending upon the information selected, though, the message can become distorted. **Distortion** refers to how people consciously or unconsciously change messages.

Distortion is usually not deliberate. People unconsciously pass along only information they feel others need. Often they leave out important data. Distortion may be deliberate, however, for self-enhancement or self-protection. For example, an employee may tell a supervisor about a machine breakdown but not admit that he or she did not oil the machine regularly. Or a manager may give an employee a very good rating because she likes him, even though the worker's performance may be only average.

Distortion can also occur because people often "hear" what they want to hear. We all bring our own perspectives to any communication situation. We filter messages we receive through our own system of beliefs and experience. Therefore, sometimes what we understand the sender to say was not at all what the sender meant. Receivers don't necessarily have to agree with the message, but they have a responsibility to use feedback to try to understand it as the sender intended.

■ CHANNELS OF COMMUNICATION

A **channel of communication** is the means by which the message is conveyed. The three major channels are oral, written, and non-verbal.

ORAL COMMUNICATION   In the opening story we learned that Erica's schedule for the next business day is nearly filled with oral communications. Speaking with employees, attending meetings, and receiving and making phone calls consume a great deal of a manager's time. Day-to-day communications require frequent contact with people on a one-to-one basis. That contact may be formal, as when Erica interviews a potential employee, or it may be informal, as when she chats with another employee about the company picnic. Giving employees oral instructions is an especially common and significant task. How well managers communicate determines in great part how high they rise on the management ladder.

WRITTEN COMMUNICATION   Written business communications take many forms. The most common are short memos, e-mails, formal reports, and letters. Figure 10-3 lists some common uses of business letters. Other written communications include manuals, invoices, telephone message reminders, and even notes. Written communications sent electronically include e-mails, faxes, and postings on electronic bulletin boards.

To communicate effectively in writing, senders should compose messages using precise, unambiguous word choice and proper grammar. The messages should also be concise. Long or unnecessary messages contribute to information overload. In turn, information overload slows decision making and becomes an obstacle to effective use of work time. Written messages may also include the use of psychology. For example, good news should appear early in a message, and bad news should appear later, after the explanation.

ELECTRONIC COMMUNICATION   E-mail has changed the way we communicate. Yearly over a trillion e-mail messages replace what otherwise would be paper correspondence. Evidence of the growth of e-mail is the great decline in messages previously sent through the U.S. Postal System. Electronic mail is popular because it lowers communication costs, minimizes paper handling, speeds communications and decision-making, and improves office productivity. Because of its rapid growth and widespread use, businesses have adopted policies and practices that address e-mail use.

Some Uses for Business Letters

- request credit from suppliers
- give and refuse credit to customers
- collect overdue accounts from customers
- request product catalogs from suppliers
- order merchandise from suppliers
- send information customers requested
- acknowledge and fill orders from customers
- ask for and make adjustments in customers' orders
- refuse adjustments in customers' orders
- persuade others to take action
- convince others about an idea
- sell goods and services
- congratulate others
- thank people for tasks performed
- request information about job applicants
- request interviews with job applicants
- hire or reject job applicants

FIGURE 10-3

Business letters have many purposes.

E-Mail Policies. Some businesses establish e-mail policies to protect the organization, business partners, employees, and customers. Typically such policies state that employees should use e-mail only for job-related matters, with occasional exceptions. In fact, businesses can track all inbound and outbound messages and read them if they want. Employees should not use e-mail for personal purposes, such as contacting friends outside the organization or participating in chat groups. In general, employee communications cannot be considered private, because all employee actions represent the firm. Companies like General Electric remind employees as they log on that most Internet and e-mail use is solely for business tasks and all activity may be recorded and reviewed.

Also, e-mail should not be considered private, because outsiders can access it. For that reason, some organizations install software programs that can automatically self-destruct messages after a designated time, limit the number of times a message can be opened and read, and prevent the forwarding of messages.

Protecting the company from lawsuits is too critical to be left to chance. Jokes, off-color stories, and flame messages reflect negatively on the company image. A **flame** is an electronic message that contains abusive, threatening, or offensive content that may violate company policy or public law. Abusive sexual language, for example, can lead to a sexual harassment lawsuit by offended employees. Abusers are subject to dismissal and firms may be sued for permitting harassment situations to exist.

A recent survey of 900 employers by the American Management Association found that 35 percent do one or more of the following: monitor employee voice mail, phone calls, e-mail, and computer hard drives, and videotape employees at their jobs.

E-Mail Practices. E-mail volume can be quite heavy. Information overload is a common complaint of employees in information-intensive jobs. They need strategies for processing large amounts of mail efficiently. Different avenues are available for doing so. Important mail from superiors and co-workers deserves priority. Some mail need not be read at all, such as spam. **Spam** is unsolicited advertising that finds its way into e-mail boxes. Most common e-mail programs allow users to sort incoming messages by sender, subject line, or whatever they specify. Thus, users can have all messages from the boss grouped together, so they give these top priority. Spam from unknown senders can be grouped together for quick disposal. Productive employees set aside certain times of the day to send or read e-mail, so that this task does not interfere with other priority tasks.

Writing and responding to e-mail deserve the same courtesy that other written mail deserves. Good business writing requires that messages have a meaningful subject line as well as a pleasant but business-like tone that gets to the point quickly and ends graciously. Most messages should be short, but some may have attachments, such as a tables, charts, or diagrams. Users often write e-mail messages hurriedly, and do not carefully craft them. Furthermore, employees may not realize that e-mail, like letters, are written documents that can be used for legal purposes.

A possible weakness of e-mail, as opposed to phone or in-person conversations, is the lack of facial expressions and other gestures that show emotions. However, senders can express some common emotions through emoticons. **Emoticons** are facial expressions created with keyboard symbols and used to express feeling in an e-mail message. Figure 10-4 shows some common emoticons. To see the expressions, look at the emoticons sideways. Users should be careful not to overuse emoticons, especially in business correspondence. Too many emoticons can make the message seem unprofessional.

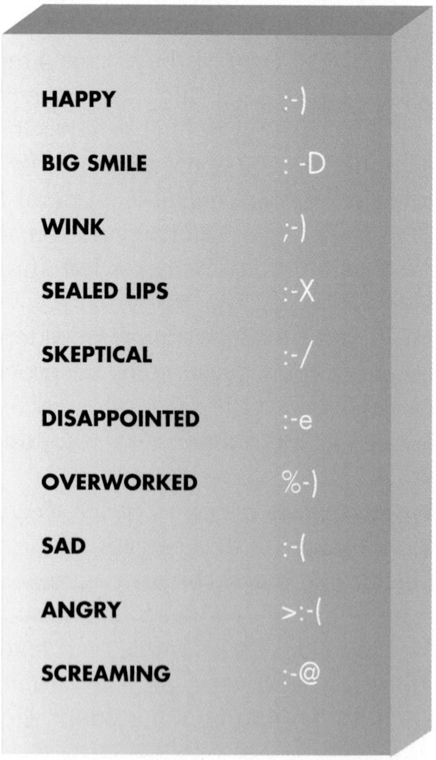

Each e-mail message should follow good

FIGURE 10-4

Emoticons provide e-mail users a way to convey feelings.

HAPPY	:-)
BIG SMILE	:-D
WINK	;-)
SEALED LIPS	:-X
SKEPTICAL	:-/
DISAPPOINTED	:-e
OVERWORKED	%-)
SAD	:-(
ANGRY	>:-(
SCREAMING	:-@

writing guidelines. Writers should construct sentences properly, without spelling errors. They should not include gossip or nasty comments. Carelessly prepared messages reflect negatively on the writer and the organization.

NON-VERBAL COMMUNICATION

Delivering messages by means other than speaking or writing is called **non-verbal communications.** Flashing lights, stop signs, and sirens are examples of physical ways to communicate. Even colors, such as in traffic lights (green,

ILLUSTRATION 10-2

Body language may get the message across better than the spoken word. What message is this businesswoman sending?

yellow, and red), signal messages—go, caution, and stop. Non-verbal communication also appears in written documents in the form of charts, diagrams, and pictures. People also give non-verbal messages through body movements. "Body language," as this is sometimes called, may appear as frowns, smiles, posture, hand or body movements, or presence or absence of eye contact. Non-verbal messages convey meaning as much as verbal messages do.

Managers should be aware of the non-verbal messages they convey to others and that others convey to them. These messages are often given unconsciously. Sometimes a non-verbal message confirms or contradicts a verbal message. For example, what impression would Erica get if tomorrow's job applicant said, "I am extremely interested in the position," but came unprepared for the interview and wore jeans and a dirty T-shirt? If you were interviewing this person, which message would you believe—the verbal or non-verbal one? Actions often speak louder than words.

■ CORPORATE COMMUNICATIONS

Each business has its own internal atmosphere that influences the way formal and informal communications occur. In this section, you will learn how communication networks influence the communication process. You will also learn how to conduct effective meetings.

CORPORATE CULTURE

As you learned in Chapter 4, culture is shared values, beliefs, and behavior patterns of groups of people. The group may be a corporation, a nation, or any other organized group. An organization, such as a corporation, develops its own corporate culture or personality. Factors such as the type of business, personality of its leaders, and its operating procedures create this corporate culture, which members understand.

The culture of a corporation influences the communication climate. Cultures differ widely among firms. Cultures may be very closed, very open, or somewhere in between. A closed culture is one that relies on top-down decision making and adheres to numerous rules and strict disciplining for violating established procedures. Rigid rule-making and authoritarian leadership can breed distrust and secrecy while discouraging creativity and decision making at lower levels. In such organizations, communications tend to be quite formal. Experts refer to this type of organization as having a closed communication system.

When trust and confidence prevail in employees, an organization is said to have an open communication system. This type of culture encourages creativity and problem solving at all levels and supports communication and information sharing. Trust, supportiveness, risk taking, and decision making influence whether an employee will like or dislike working for a company. In turn, these factors help determine how productive employees will be.

Most organizations have neither a fully open nor closed culture. Sometimes a business may change its culture. A comfortable culture for one person, however, may not be comfortable for another. Some employees prefer a culture with primarily an open communication system, while others prefer a culture with primarily a closed communication system. Employees often change jobs in search of an organization that has a set of beliefs, values, and practices suited to their needs.

COMMUNICATION NETWORKS

A **communication network** is the structure through which information flows in a business. Communication networks can be formal or informal.

FORMAL NETWORKS   A **formal communication network** is the system of official channels that carry organizationally approved messages. These channels generally follow the reporting relationships in the firm. Formal communication flows upward, downward, and across the organization in a prescribed manner. Typically, certain information, such as budget allocations, flows downward from top-level managers to lower-level managers. Other information, such as requests for budget expenditures, flows from the bottom to the top of the organization.

Upward communication includes oral and written reports from lower level to upper-level managers. Usually, upper-level managers rely on lower-level managers for information that deals with new or unusual problems, the quality of employee performance, and the way employees feel about their jobs and the company. Supervisors receive upward communication from their subordinates about such things as project status and suggestions for making a task more efficient.

Organizations with closed, rather than open, communications are less likely to benefit from upward communication. Upward communication is subject to distortion, especially in corporate cultures that are relatively closed. Supervisors, for example, might withhold or distort upward-flowing information when problems appear to reflect negatively on their performance. On the other hand, a supervisor might exaggerate information about successes. In a closed culture, employees often fear revealing negative information and avoid making honest criticisms.

Downward communication in organizations occurs mainly by memos, e-mails, reports, and manuals. To be effective, this information should be timely and clear. In organizations with closed communications, there is often no opportunity for feedback, because information does not flow upward easily. However, in open cultures, employees receive downward-flowing information at meetings and their feedback is welcome.

Lateral communication flows horizontally or across the organization. For example, the production manager in one plant might want to know what problems other production managers face. Perhaps common problems could be solved jointly. However, many organizations do not have easy and fast channels for such communications. In a business with an open corporate culture, lateral communications are more likely to exist. One communication expert has estimated that 80 percent of poor management decisions occur because of ineffective communications.

CAREER CONNECTION

COMPUTER SYSTEMS ANALYST

Computer systems analyst is expected to be one of the fastest-growing occupations in the first decade of the 2000s. The employment of computing professionals is expected to increase rapidly as technologies become more sophisticated and organizations continue to adopt and integrate them.

Systems analysts use their knowledge and skills to solve computer problems and enable computer technology to meet the individual needs of an organization. This may include planning and developing new computer systems or devising ways to apply existing systems' resources. Analysts work to help an organization realize the maximum benefit from its investment in equipment, personnel, and business processes. Most systems analysts generally work with a specific type of system, depending on the type of organization they work for—for example, business, accounting, or financial systems.

Given the technology available today, telecommuting is becoming more common for computer professionals. Often work can be done from remote locations using modems, laptops, e-mail, and through the Internet.

While there is no universally accepted way to prepare for a job as a computer professional because employers' preferences depend on the work to be done, a bachelor's degree is a prerequisite for most employers. Relevant work experience is also very important.

For more career information about systems analysts, check your library or the Internet for resources.

INFORMAL NETWORKS   Like formal communication networks, informal networks exist in all organizations. **Informal communication networks** are the unofficial ways that employees share information in an organization. The most common informal networks include small informal groups and the grapevine. Informal networks rely heavily on interpersonal communications and e-mail.

A great deal of communicating occurs among small informal groups, especially among employees who get along well together. These employees may or may not have the same supervisors, but often they do. They share information about the organization, assist one another in solving work problems, and look after one another. Members may even support one another when conflicts arise with other employees. Most employees belong to a small informal group.

Managers should be aware of informal groups. Often informal groups have more influence than managers do over the behavior of individual workers. It is extremely important that informal groups support the efforts of the entire business. If they do not, informal groups can interfere with business goals and, in turn, hurt morale and decrease productivity. Managers often work closely with informal group leaders to obtain support and to test new ideas.

An extensive amount of organizational communications occurs in an unofficial way through interpersonal relationships. Employees working side by side, for example, generally talk about their jobs and about personal matters. These conversations are normal and usually do not interfere with work. Employees also talk together on breaks, in the hall, or around the drinking fountain.

The informal transmission of information among workers is called the **grapevine.** Informal messages travel quickly through the grapevine and can be distorted, because they are often based on unofficial, partial, or incorrect information. That is why grapevine messages are often labeled rumors. Very often, however, grapevines convey accurate messages. For example, when a formal memo announces that a manager has just retired for "health reasons," the grapevine may provide the actual reason. The manager may have been asked to quit but was given the opportunity to resign voluntarily. When Erica Komuro calls Sabrina in Accounting, she may also learn that the rumor about the vice president's resignation is true.

Generally, managers should not interfere with grapevines. Grapevines often fill the social needs of workers to communicate about their work lives. Only when a grapevine message is inaccurate and negatively affects company business should managers attempt to correct the situation.

CONDUCTING EFFECTIVE MEETINGS

Meetings are a common way for employees to share information, discuss problems, and make decisions. Managers often prefer meetings, because open communication encourages discussion and yields feed-

1. Have a good reason for calling a meeting.
2. Develop a specific agenda and stick to it.
3. Decide who should and who should not attend.
4. Schedule the meeting at a convenient time and place.
5. Start and stop the meeting on time.
6. Encourage communications by arranging the seating so that participants face one another.
7. Summarize the results at the end of the meeting.

FIGURE 10-5

Suggestions for Running Effective Meetings

QUESTION 14
Exam 4

back that helps in decision making. Employees doing the hands-on work often have good ideas about how to improve their work quality and efficiency. However, meetings also have disadvantages. The chief disadvantage is the excessive time meetings take. Good managers overcome this weakness by careful planning and by following suggestions such as those shown in Figure 10-5.

A second major problem with meetings occurs because of differences among those who attend the meetings. For example, an outspoken person may tend to dominate, while a quiet person may say nothing. Neither situation is desirable. The person who leads the meeting should encourage but control discussions, so that the group hears and discusses all ideas. Two methods used to encourage group thinking and problem solving are the nominal group technique and brainstorming.

NOMINAL GROUP TECHNIQUE The **nominal group technique (NGT)** is a group problem-solving method in which group members write down and evaluate ideas to be shared with the group. For example, assume a manager needs to solve a long-standing problem. The manager begins by stating the problem and then follows the steps described in Figure 10-6.

QUESTION 10
Exam 4

The NGT encourages each group member to think about the problem, and it gives the quiet person and the outspoken person equal

QUESTION 16
Exam 4

1. Present the problem to be resolved to group members.
2. Distribute blank cards and, without discussion, ask members to write possible solutions by using a different card for each solution.
3. Read solutions from the cards and display for all to see.
4. Discuss each solution listed.
5. Distribute blank cards and ask members to write their three best solutions on separate cards.
6. Tabulate and display results.
7. Select the solution receiving the most agreement and present it to the group leader.

FIGURE 10-6

Steps in Using the Nominal Group Technique

opportunity to be heard. Private voting encourages employees to choose the best solutions rather than spend time defending their own suggestions. As a result, this technique has been very effective.

BRAINSTORMING Problems arise in business for which prior solutions do not exist or are no longer acceptable. One technique for handling such situations is by brainstorming. **Brainstorming** is a group discussion technique used to generate as many ideas as possible for solving a problem. A group leader presents a problem and asks group members to offer any solution that comes to mind. Even wild and imaginative ideas are encouraged. The group should make no attempt to judge any ideas as good or bad while brainstorming is underway. Only after participants have identified all possible solutions should they begin to judge usefulness. Often, an idea that appeared to be impractical or unusual when first presented may become the best solution to the problem. Brainstorming is frequently used to deal with problems that need especially creative solutions, such as when generating new product ideas and creating advertisements.

COMMUNICATION PROBLEMS

Managers deal with a variety of communication problems. Some problems that challenge the communication skills of managers involve resolving conflicts and handling cross-cultural communications effectively.

DEALING WITH CONFLICT

At times, people disagree with each other. Most job-related disagreements are likely to be temporary and easy to settle. Disagreements become a concern to a business when they lead to conflict. **Conflict** is interference by one person with the achievement of another person's goals. Conflicts usually occur between two people, but they may also occur between an individual and a group, or between groups. Because conflicts are sometimes an obstacle to job performance, managers must deal with conflicts.

DESIRABLE CONFLICT A small amount of conflict is sometimes beneficial, because it may challenge employees and stimulate new ideas. For example, the advertising manager may decide to budget as little as possible to advertise a particular product, while the sales manager may have decided to try to boost sales for that particular product through increased advertising. At this point conflict exists because the goals set by each manager differ. However, this type of conflict can lead to a healthy discussion of how much to spend on advertising and how best to advertise to produce the highest sales at the lowest advertising cost. The result can lead to the achievement of a goal that is best for the business.

When employees discuss and resolve their conflicting goals, the organization can benefit. However, when conflicting goals are not resolved, long-term problems often result. If the sales and advertising managers went ahead with their individual plans, money would be wasted and sales would be lost.

ILLUSTRATION 10-3

If handled properly, conflicts can be beneficial and productive. How do you handle conflict with another person?

UNDESIRABLE CONFLICT

While some conflict in organizations may be healthy, too much conflict can be harmful. Undesirable conflict results when the actions of any person or group interfere with the goals of the organization. If, in the preceding example, the sales manager became resentful of the advertising manager and undermined the company's budget goals by deliberately overspending the amount agreed upon for the product, undesirable conflict would result. Employees who dislike others and carry grudges often cause problems for an organization. Therefore, undesirable conflicts should be resolved as soon as possible.

RESOLVING CONFLICT Conflicts can be resolved in various ways. Since each situation differs, managers must decide which type of strategy will best resolve each conflict.

Avoidance Strategy. One strategy used to resolve conflict is to take a neutral position or to agree with another person's position even though it differs from your personal belief. This approach avoids the conflict. One manager may decide to accept the goal of another manager, or to avoid expressing an opposing opinion about the goal. When a conflict is relatively unimportant, the avoidance strategy may be the best approach. However, if a disagreement involves important issues, avoidance is not a good strategy. It can often lead to resentment.

Compromise Strategy. A second way to resolve conflict is to seek a compromise. Everyone involved in a conflict agrees to a mutually acceptable solution. Often, a compromise grows out of a thorough discussion of the goals and the best way to achieve those goals. This strategy is better than avoidance, because it usually leads to a workable solution, since everyone involved personally contributes to the decision.

FACTS AND FIGURES

Companies experiencing workplace violence report a dramatic increase in employee turnover and an equally dramatic drop in employee morale. Since most employees feel that it is the employer's duty to provide a safe work environment, workers feel betrayed when a violent incident occurs at work. The ultimate consequences of turnover and low morale are hiring and training expenses and decreased productivity.

Also, people are more likely to support a compromise solution that they have helped to develop.

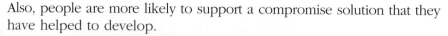

Win/Lose Strategy. The most dangerous approach used to resolve conflict is a win/lose strategy. A win/lose strategy is one in which no one compromises, thereby resulting in one person winning and one losing. A win/lose strategy is never acceptable to everyone, although people often engage in such a strategy. Win/lose strategies interfere with the achievement of organizational goals because they often (1) take time and energy away from the main problems and issues, (2) delay decisions, (3) arouse anger that hurts human relationships, and (4) cause personal resentment, which can lead to other problems.

Because win/lose situations are destructive, managers should attempt to prevent them. Setting clear objectives that employees understand and agree on, stressing the need for cooperation in reaching objectives, and working for group decisions when special problems or disagreements arise are ways managers can avoid win/lose strategies.

■ CROSS-CULTURAL COMMUNICATION PROBLEMS

Cultures differ from country to country. A country's culture influences how its people communicate, just as corporate culture does within organizations. When doing business abroad, companies face communication barriers created by language, cultural, and non-verbal differences.

LANGUAGE DIFFERENCES Few American managers speak a foreign language fluently. However, doing so does not solve all problems when

ILLUSTRATION 10-4

What kinds of communication barriers might companies face when doing business abroad?

someone is transferred to another country. The people of most nations realize that learning a new language is difficult. But they are more than willing to help foreigners learn. They are especially impressed when someone who does not know their language makes a noble effort to learn. Many corporations now provide intensive language training for managers assigned to foreign branches. Knowledge of the social customs and education, legal, and political systems are included in the instructions.

Joint ventures between American and foreign firms often reveal language problems. A successful joint venture between Ford Motor Co. and the Japanese Mazda Motors Corp. provides an example of overcoming language difficulties. The president of Mazda estimates that 20 percent of the meaning of a conversation with Ford leaders is lost between him and the interpreters. Another 20 percent is lost between the interpreters and the Ford leaders. Working with only about two-thirds understanding, the Mazda president tries extra hard to make sure his message is getting through. He especially believes people should meet face-to-face and talk freely.

CULTURAL DIFFERENCES People from other countries place different values on such things as family, status, and power. Countries value families differently. In India, for example, providing jobs for male family members in a business is more important than earning a profit. Humor differs worldwide, too. In addition, accepted practices in one country may be impolite elsewhere. For example, American business people generally like to start and end meetings on time. In Japan and certain other countries, this practice would be considered rude rather than businesslike.

NON-VERBAL DIFFERENCES Great differences exist in the area of non-verbal communications, especially body language. For example, how close one stands when talking to someone else differs from one country to another. For most conversations, Americans stand two to three feet apart, whereas Middle Eastern people stand much closer. Even colors have different meanings. In Western countries, black is often associated with death, but in Latin American countries, death is represented by white and purple. A handshake also varies from place to place. In Spain, it should last from five to seven shakes, but the French prefer one single shake.

Because differences exist among nations, executives prefer to conduct extremely important business transactions in a formal manner. Usually, that means greater use of written reports and expert translators. For oral translation services by phone, long-distance telephone firms such as AT&T provide an 800-number to assist callers. However, for day-to-day international operations, managers must learn to understand the cultural and communication practices of other nations.

FACTS AND FIGURES

Listening is considered both a sign of politeness and a valuable skill in business negotiations in Japan. Japanese often think North Americans need to listen more attentively, not talk as much, and certainly not interrupt when someone else is speaking.

■IMPROVING ORGANIZATIONAL COMMUNICATIONS

Good managers are usually good communicators. Some ways to improve communication are discussed next.

■ ENCOURAGE TWO-WAY COMMUNICATIONS

Small businesses provide for plenty of two-way communication between owners and employees. As companies get larger, however, a shift to one-way communications often occurs for efficiency purposes. When this happens, problems arise because valuable feedback from employees and customers is reduced. Good managers establish plans to obtain feedback even when they are extremely busy. Some managers, however, discourage two-way communications because they feel uncomfortable with it and because it is time-consuming. For example, one boss in a firm fired an employee by e-mail, even though the person's office was located next door. Organizations that encourage managers to consciously engage in two-way communications are often more successful than those that do not.

■ LISTEN ACTIVELY

Two-way communications assure feedback. Effective listening results in effective feedback. Frequently, employees have questions and encounter problems on the job. They need to talk to someone who listens carefully. Hearing and listening are not the same. Most people can hear when someone speaks, but they may not pay attention to the message. Listening involves hearing and understanding. Good listeners make

ILLUSTRATION 10-5

New managers often spend time listening to as many employee points of view as possible before making corporate changes. What kinds of questions would you ask employees before making such changes?

every effort to practice the rules of good listening shown in Figure 10-7 to make certain that they received the messages accurately.

■ FACILITATE UPWARD COMMUNICATION

In large organizations, upward communication is sometimes neglected. Managers may not want to hear complaints or deal with suggestions

Rule and Reason Behind the Rule

FIGURE 10-7

Ten Rules for Good Listening

1. Stop talking!

You cannot listen if you are talking.

2. Put the talker at ease.

Help a person feel free to talk; create a permissive environment.

3. Show a talker that you want to listen.

Look and act interested; listen to understand, not to oppose.

4. Remove distractions.

Don't doodle, tap, or shuffle papers; shut the door if necessary to acheive quiet.

5. Empathize with talkers.

Try to see the other person's point of view.

6. Be patient.

Allow plenty of time; do not interrupt; do not start for the door or walk away.

7. Hold your temper.

An angry person takes the wrong meaning from words.

8. Go easy on argument and criticism.

These put people on the defensive and may cause them to "clam up" or become angry. Do not argue—even if you win, you lose.

9. Ask questions.

This encourages a talker and shows that you are listening. It helps to develop points further.

10. Stop talking!

This is first and last, because all other guides depend on it. You cannot do an effective listening job while you are talking. Remember that:
- Nature gave people two ears but only one tongue, which is a gentle hint that they should listen more than they talk.
- Listening requires two ears, one for meaning and one for feeling.
- Decision makers who do not listen have less information for making sound decisions.

because they require time. To make certain that upward communications occur, some businesses ask managers to use specific techniques.

QUESTION 6
Exam 4

One technique is called "management by walking around." Managers leave their offices from time to time and make trips through the working areas. While doing this, they chat with employees about various problems and conditions.

Another practice is for managers to encourage employees to meet with them when they have concerns. To control the time this "open door policy" takes, some managers restrict the practice to one hour per week when employees can make appointments. Suggestion boxes have been used for many years and have great value in encouraging communications.

No technique is better than regular meetings with employees. Some firms select a certain number of employees from different departments and organizational levels to meet with top managers on a regular basis. The manager informs them about important company matters and invites questions and ideas. Studies have shown that employees who are informed about their companies have stronger positive feelings than those who are not. These top-level managers benefit by getting feedback from people throughout the company.

■ SELECT COMMUNICATION CHANNELS CAREFULLY

When managers want to communicate with others, they should carefully select an appropriate communication channel. Generally, when a manager must reprimand an employee or settle a dispute, the oral communication channel is best. The oral channel is needed to explain the reason for the reprimand or to work out an acceptable solution to a dispute.

QUESTION 8
Exam 4

The written communication channel is best when managers want to communicate information requiring future action or to communicate information of a general nature, such as a new policy or a revised operating procedure. Such matters should be put in writing for later reference. Managers should follow up on information provided in writing, because it serves as a reminder that the information is important and it provides an opportunity for the receiver to ask questions. E-mail is a good way to follow up because it is fast, easy, and provides immediate feedback. E-mail is not a good substitute for oral communication in situations that call for face-to-face discussion.

In some situations, two channels of communication work best— first oral and then written. Managers should use both channels when they want to (1) give an immediate order, (2) announce a new policy, (3) contact a supervisor about work problems, or (4) compliment an employee for excellent work. In most of these situations, the information is best delivered orally on a one-to-one basis, which personalizes it and allows for immediate feedback. The written channel then allows for reinforcement and creates a record of the event.

ETHICAL ISSUES

COMMUNICATING TO CHANGE ATTITUDES

Monsanto frequently ranks as one of America's two hundred largest firms. While the public may not recognize the name, many recognize at least one product—NutraSweet. NutraSweet is Monsanto's brand of the sugar substitute aspartame often used in diet foods and drinks. At any grocery store, read the "contents" portion of labels on canned and packaged foods, and you will see how popular aspartame has become.

Aspartame received bad press in its early days and still does in spite of the fact that the Food and Drug Administration, American Diabetes Association, and other groups declared it safe for public consumption. Research by organizations other than Monsanto have also found it safe. Critics, however, think aspartame is not safe. Some think it may lead to headaches, blindness, cancer, and other problems, though these assertions are not supported by scientific evidence. Yet, Monsanto continues to receive complaints in spite of its extensive communication efforts to convince the public otherwise.

Although American-made products must list sugar substitutes, that is not true in some countries. In Europe and Asia, for example, manufacturers are not required to list sugar substitutes. Simply listing "sweetener" is acceptable, whether it is sugar, aspartame, or something else. This practice arises for economic reasons. For example, aspartame is easier and cheaper to ship, is subjected to fewer trade barriers and tariffs, is easily available when there is a sugar shortage, and is cheaper when sugar prices are high.

Monsanto makes other controversial products that have also received public criticism. Those products involve biotechnology—the genetic altering of crops that we eat. Examples include modifying one or two genes in soybeans, potatoes, and corn to make them more resistant to insects and diseases. While scientific experts find biotechnology acceptable, critics reject genetic altering and want it stopped or tightly controlled. With a growing population worldwide, how can farmers increase crop output and be more productive? Biotechnology can increase crop yields. Again, Monsanto has spent millions of dollars persuading the public that its new products, which are approved by the Food and Drug Administration and the American Dietetic Association, are not injurious to human health.

THINK CRITICALLY

1. How does the public's resistance to Monsanto's NutraSweet differ from the resistance to its biotechnology products?
2. Is it unethical to exclude aspartame from the contents of prepared foods in other countries?
3. Would Americans find it acceptable if the contents of food and drink products simply listed "sweetener" rather than "sugar" or "aspartame"?
4. Investigate Monsanto's success with its public communications efforts. Obtain information from your library or visit Web sites such as www.monsanto. com. Make a report to your class.

CHAPTER CONCEPTS

■ Managers spend much of their time communicating by writing, speaking, and listening. Communication involves creating, sending, receiving, and interpreting messages with the knowledge that each step in the communication process includes potential barriers.

■ Corporate culture involves the shared values, beliefs, and behavior of an organization. The culture is established by its CEO and managers, and it influences the way people communicate within the firm. Cultures may be (1) entirely open with extensive interactive communication among all organizational members, (2) entirely closed with dominantly downward communication, or (3) a combination of open and closed communication. An open culture exists more often in today's successful firms and is characterized by trust, support, and a positive outlook among employees.

■ Communications in organizations follow both formal and informal networks. Formal communication networks are official company channels, such as between managers and their employees. Informal communication networks are communications that occur among informal groups or through the grapevine.

■ Managers must deal with many types of problems that challenge their communication skills, such as conflicts and communication across cultures. They must also learn to run meetings effectively by using techniques such as the nominal group technique and brainstorming to arrive at solutions to business problems.

■ Good managers are generally good communicators. They listen effectively, facilitate upward communications, and choose the appropriate communication channels for their messages.

BUILD VOCABULARY POWER

Define the following terms and concepts.

1. communication
2. feedback
3. distraction
4. distortion
5. channel of communication
6. flame
7. spam
8. emoticons
9. non-verbal communications
10. communication network
11. formal communication network
12. informal communication networks
13. grapevine
14. nominal group technique (NGT)
15. brainstorming
16. conflict

REVIEW FACTS

1. How much time do managers spend each day communicating?
2. Why is communication referred to as a two-way process?
3. Name three problems that can occur in a business when poor communications exist.

4. What are two major barriers to communications?
5. Name the major channels used in business for communicating.
6. How do emoticons overcome a weakness of e-mail as a means of communication?
7. What is "body language"?
8. What are some characteristics of a business that has a closed culture?
9. Are messages that flow through the grapevine often incorrect?
10. What three strategies can a manager use to resolve conflicts?
11. Give five suggestions for running an effective meeting.
12. Would the nominal group technique or brainstorming be more effective in generating a large number of creative ideas for solving a problem?
13. List three differences about which American managers must be aware when transacting business in other countries.
14. How is listening different from hearing?
15. In what types of situations should managers use both oral and written channels of communication?

DISCUSS IDEAS

1. Discuss the importance of feedback in two-way communications.
2. Explain how a grammar error in a memo might be considered a distraction and thus a barrier to communications.
3. Distortion is not always unconsciously done. Why might employees consciously distort information? Do you think such behavior is ethical? Explain.
4. Describe the psychology behind why good news should be stated early in a written message and why bad news should be delayed somewhat.
5. A manager was enjoying giving a talk to a group of young people about business. An audience member asked the manager whether he believed in open communications. The manager looked uncomfortable with the question, snapped a fast "yes," and quickly asked, "Any other questions?" Compare the oral and non-verbal message of the manager.
6. Discuss the main factors that help to determine the culture of an organization.
7. Discuss what strategy you would use to help resolve a conflict situation between two employees who always disagree on how a task should be handled.
8. Ann and Susan became friends at work and often e-mailed each other during the day about personal matters. One day Susan sent a negative message about her manager, but it accidentally was sent to a higher-level manager, who asked Susan for an explanation. What would you do as that manager if Susan had violated company policy prohibiting such messages?

9. Although cultures differ from country to country, how can cultures differ within a country such as the United States?
10. How might busy managers follow a policy of encouraging effective listening?

ANALYZE INFORMATION

1. From Figure 10-1, determine the percentage of time managers spend each workday (a) listening, (b) speaking, (c) reading, and (d) writing. Also, determine the total percentage of time that they spend in communicating and in other activities.
2. One type of non-verbal communication involves the use of body language. When your teacher directs you, demonstrate five different messages by using only your hands and/or arms. Identify emoticons that match any of your five messages.
3. With the help of your teacher, complete the following activities that show communication breakdowns. Find a picture from a magazine that shows action, such as someone running, dancing, or playing a musical instrument. Then, ask for three, four, or five volunteers. Tell one volunteer to stay at the front of the class and ask the other volunteers to go beyond hearing and viewing distance. Now follow these steps:
   a. Explain to the first volunteer that you will allow one minute to study the action picture, which the person must then describe to the second volunteer. (Show the picture for one minute to the volunteer and then conceal the picture.)
   b. Call in the second volunteer, and ask the first volunteer to describe the picture in as much detail as possible. Two-way communications are acceptable.
   c. Call the third volunteer and ask the second volunteer to relay the description just received. Continue this process until all volunteers have had a chance to listen to the description and repeat what they heard.
   d. Show the picture to the volunteers and the class, and ask if the scene is what they thought was being described.
   e. Summarize by a discussion or written report what you learned about the communication process and how communication breakdowns occur.
4. Assume that you are working for a business that has many new young part-time workers. Many of the workers are often late or absent. As a result, other employees must work longer hours and are often called in on weekends. Divide into groups and conduct group meetings to solve the problem, using the nominal group technique. Present the best solutions to your teacher, who will serve as the manager of the work group. When done, discuss how well the NGT worked.

5. LaToya put the following idea in her company's suggestion box: "Rather than hire a new full-time worker at $15.00 per hour to handle our increased business, hire two half-time workers at $10.00 per hour. Then if business slows later, we can cut back to one half-time worker or no workers."

   a. As the manager, write LaToya a note saying that her suggestion has been accepted and she will earn 20 percent of one year's saving for the idea.

   b. Assume one year went by and that one half-time employee worked 860 hours and the second worked 600 hours. A full-time employee would have worked 2,000 hours. How much will LaToya receive for her suggestion?

6. Divide into small groups. For this project, you may interact with your group only by e-mail. Brainstorm a list of e-mail do's and don'ts appropriate for a workplace setting. Using your group's ideas, compose an e-mail policy for your workplace. E-mail your group's policy to your teacher.

7. As a class, identify an important school issue on which students strongly disagree. Then hold a class conflict-resolution meeting. Use a brainstorming technique to generate ideas for resolving the conflict. Then use a compromise strategy to arrive at a solution.

SOLVE BUSINESS PROBLEMS

CASE 10-1

Lauren Lemaster works at the headquarters office for a major Internet corporation that has offices in five countries. The company has a strict set of rules regarding the use of e-mail. Hackers often try to break into the operating system to damage it and that naturally hurts business.

The CEO sends all newly hired employees the following message: "Be careful what you say to others, especially when using e-mail with other employees. A year ago a hacker learned that we were planning to buy another business that would increase the value of the company. He found out about our intended purchase and took the idea to a competitor, so we lost 'big' on that failed operation. For reasons like this, we require you to sign the attached oath. The oath states that if an employee is responsible in any way for inside information getting to the outside, that employee will be released immediately." Without further thought, Lauren signed, but that was two years ago.

Yesterday, on her lunch hour Lauren sent a secret e-mail message to her best friend, Douglas, who likes to buy stock in Internet companies when they do something new and exciting. Lauren's message said: "Douglas, I learned that my company has its eye on Dawson and Donaldson, Inc. Keep it to yourself. Hopefully this will repay the favor you did to help me get this job. Trash this message after reading it. Lauren."

Douglas bought stock in the company and shared the message with several friends, who also bought stock. Then he destroyed the message. And within 24 hours, the stock doubled in price. However, Lauren's boss called her in and fired her on the spot for having violated company policy.

Think Critically:

1. Was the company's Internet policy too severe? Why or why not? Because Lauren wrote the e-mail on her lunch hour, is she actually in violation of company policy?
2. How did the company find out about Lauren's e-mail message?
3. Does Lauren have any privacy rights that would enable her to sue the company for the loss of her job? Explain.
4. Was Lauren as unethical as Douglas was? And what responsibility does Douglas have for Lauren's plight?
5. How would the ten rules for good listening apply when Lauren and Douglas meet to discuss what happened?

CASE 10-2

As a former regional manager for Graphix International, Seth McClaren was promoted and transferred to the Philadelphia headquarters several years ago. A close friend, Josh Berry, manages the company's regional office in Atlanta. Josh arrived in Philadelphia today, along with other regional managers. At tomorrow's meeting, the latest procedures for submitting monthly reports will be explained by the new top managers. Seth called Josh and invited him to dinner this evening to discuss concerns about changes going on. After dinner the following conversation occurs:

Seth: *Tomorrow's a big meeting. The new president and the two new vice presidents will be there to explain the new reporting procedures.*

Josh: *Was something wrong with the old method? It worked fine for my office. We do the reports according to the rules. We hear from headquarters only when something isn't done right.*

Seth: *The new managers are different. They like meetings and lots of contact with employees. They even stop by my office every few weeks to chat. They seem friendly . . . even invited me to stop by their offices if I have a problem. Nothing like the former managers! You never saw them and never heard from them unless something went wrong. Then threatening memos would come from all directions.*

Josh: *Is that why most of the regional managers kept clear of headquarters? The person I replaced warned me not to break any of the rules. "Just keep your nose clean," she said. "If you don't bother them, they won't bother you."*

Seth: *That's the main reason why the board of directors changed the top managers. The new managers expect good work, but they also seem to want the employees and managers to discuss problems. They even want us to suggest solutions. Imagine that! Some of us aren't sure whether to trust them yet. We're afraid if we make one mistake, we'll be fired.*

Josh: *They seem to be practicing what they preach, Seth. The Houston regional manager stuck her neck out and made a suggestion, and a vice president flew down to talk with her. The grapevine said he made a real big thing over the idea. Her picture is in the newsletter that just came out. The*

newsletter has plenty of information about the business and about her suggestion.

Seth: *That's what I mean, Josh. The way these new people operate . . . it's different. I'm not sure I like it. The new monthly report even has a place in it where you can state complaints and make suggestions. They're going to get an earful when the next month's forms are returned. That's no way to run a business.*

Josh: *Let's give them a chance, Seth. At least they're willing to listen, which is more than you could say about the departed managers.*

Think Critically:

1. Did the corporate culture change between the old and new top management? Explain.
2. What evidence is there that the new top management will encourage or discourage upward communication?
3. Did the vice president who flew out to see the Houston regional manager regarding a suggestion for improvement use more than one channel of communication? If yes, how?
4. Did the old or the new top managers place more stress on two-way communications? Explain.
5. Will Seth be as comfortable as Josh with the new managers? Explain your answer.

PROJECT: MY BUSINESS, INC.

As a small business owner, you will be responsible for making sure communications flow smoothly within your business and with others outside your business. Unclear or poor communications can be very damaging to a new business as you work with employees, customers, other business people, and the public. You need to plan communications carefully and use effective communications whenever you interact with others.

DATA COLLECTION

1. Using newspapers, business magazines, and Internet news services, identify situations where businesses faced problems resulting from poor communications. Make a list of the types of communication problems you identify, using the following categories: communications problems with (a) employees, (b) customers, (c) other business people, (d) the public, (e) other.
2. Advertising is one method of communicating with customers. However, advertisements often do not communicate the same message to everyone. Locate three advertisements from small businesses.

If possible, find advertisements from businesses similar to your juice bar business. Show the advertisements to five different people. Record their answers to the following questions:

a What is the most important message you receive from the advertisement?

b. In general, do you believe the advertisement is effective or ineffective?

c. As a result of the advertisement, would you be more or less likely to be a customer of the business? Why?

3. As a small business owner, you are concerned that meetings with your employees be as effective as possible. Use library or Internet resources to research the topic of "rules of order" or "parliamentary procedure" in meetings. How can you apply these rules to your business?

ANALYSIS

1. Compose a letter that you would send to local health clubs and recreation centers. Use the letter to request that your juice bar be identified as the "exclusive source for juice drinks" for their facility. Make sure the letter is persuasive and offers some value or benefit to the businesses you will contact.

2. You have been asked by the local organization of retailers to make a brief presentation at their monthly luncheon meeting about your new business. Using a presentation software, prepare a five-minute presentation that describes the business, your business plan, and some of the challenges you believe you will face. Give your presentation to the class. Be prepared to defend your business plan. If possible, ask a local retailer to attend and ask questions of the presenters.